THE MILL GIRLS

With tales from hardworking Audrey and mischievous Maureen to high-spirited Doris and dedicated Marjorie, *The Mill Girls* is an evocative story of hardship and friendship from when cotton was king. Through the eyes of these northern mill girls, we are offering a fascinating glimpse into the lives of ordinary women who rallied together, nattered over the beamers and, despite the difficult working conditions, weaved, packed and laughed to keep the cotton mills spinning.

THE MILL GIRLS

THE MILL GIRLS

by

Tracy Johnson

Magna Large Print Books
Long Preston, North Yorkshire,
BD23 4ND, England.

British Library Cataloguing in Publication Data.

Johnson, Tracy
    The mill girls.

    A catalogue record of this book is
    available from the British Library

    ISBN   978-0-7505-4064-3

First published in Great Britain in 2014 by Ebury Press
an imprint of Ebury Publishing
A Random House Group Company

Published in Large Print 2015 by arrangement with
Ebury Publishing,
one of the publishers in the Random House Group Ltd.

Magna Large Print is an imprint of Library Magna Books Ltd.

Printed and bound in Great Britain by
T.J. (International) Ltd., Cornwall, PL28 8RW

For Audrey, Doris, Marjorie and Maureen

Contents

Introduction

Introduction

Being able to have the chance to meet and write about four women's lives in the mill was not only an honour but also a joy.

For someone who was born and bred in the small market town of Clitheroe, which, quite possibly, is one of the most northerly of the Lancashire cotton towns, the nature of the book struck a familiar and personal chord. By the time I was growing up, sadly, the cotton trade was well in its demise and from the fifteen mills once trading successfully there was only one left. The other mills still present around the town were now being used as car showrooms, light engineering works and supermarkets – with no trace of cotton in the air.

Funnily enough, the one surviving mill in the town, Holmes Mill, owned by weaving company James Thornber Ltd., was quite a presence in my life for many years, as it stood tall across the road from my primary school, St James.

Like every child, we were taught in school about the cotton mills, so you can imagine our excitement when we got the chance to step across the road and into a real-life one! As my teacher led the class of eager eight-year-olds around the mill, in pairs and holding hands, it was all going swimmingly until suddenly a big door slammed shut right in the path of me and a couple of others. I can't speak for the others, but I know in my child's mind I thought we'd been trapped forever in this big, noisy (and now scary) place (we hadn't, of course, and I think, just seconds later, it was reopened by our alarmed teacher). I don't think I've ever been so terrified in my life, and I'm sure our screams of terror were so loud we probably drowned out the noise from the weaving shed!

The mill also had a personal connection for me: my grandma, Greta Johnson, had worked there as a weaver. Born Greta Speak in 1919, in Clitheroe, once she had left what is now called Ribblesdale High School at 14, she was employed at Holmes Mill. She looked after five looms but twenty years later had to give up the mill due to ill health.

I regret now not asking my grandma more about her time in the mill, so through talking to Audrey, Marjorie, Doris and Maureen I've learned what it would have been like for her and all the other women of different ages – and I now appreciate how damn hard it was.

What has become apparent through speaking to the four women is that each one has a different interpretation of the mill. Doris and Maureen loved working there because of the camaraderie; Audrey used the mill as a means to an end; while Marjorie made do because it was convenient and on her doorstep. But one thing is exceptionally clear: whatever their personal feelings, the women carried on working in the mill as long as they had to and they did this for their families, because they needed the money.

Each woman may have a different story to tell, and, while their personalities differ, one thing shines through: they are all strong, proud, northern women. They have inspired me, and I feel fortunate to have met them and privileged they have chosen to share their stories with me.

Tracy Johnson
2014

Walking through the huge room towards my frame, I was ready for another day's training. It was July 1942 and it may only have been my third day at Kent Mill, in Oldham, but already I loved every minute of it.

Part One:

Doris Porter

CHAPTER ONE

Cruel Reality of Life

Walking through the huge room towards my frame, I was ready for another day's training. It was July 1942 and it may have only been my third day at Kent Mill, in Oldham, but already I loved every minute of it. It was hard work taking everything in, and standing all day long, but even at this early stage I knew I'd made the right choice in coming into the mill. I understood Mother's concerns, but the dust in the air wasn't that bad so I was sure my chest would be fine, and I knew she was just being her usual caring self. Yes, I reckoned I was going to enjoy it in here, and so far everyone had been friendly and welcoming.

But suddenly, all my thoughts got distracted when, before I knew it, two girls grabbed me and shoved me into one of the wheelers.

'What the...?!' I warbled, as a gaggle of giggles erupted. They were a couple of years older than me, about 16 or 17, but why I bothered to ask because I knew exactly what they were doing.

Soon, a few of the other workers realised what was happening and downed tools to watch. Ignoring my pleas, the girls gave the wheeler, which was a big trailer with wheels on used to carry bobbins, a great shove and off I flew along the floor – right in the direction of the office.

'Arghhh!' I screamed, as I slammed right into the boss's door. 'Oh, no!' I gulped, fearing I'd be in trouble for sure.

With that, out came the manager, but he just smiled.

'Sorry,' I sighed.

'Come on,' he smiled, raising his eyebrows and helping me out. 'You all right?'

'Yes,' I nodded.

As all the workers fell about laughing, one of the girls who'd pushed me shouted, 'Welcome to the mill!'

Shaking my head, I couldn't help but laugh. I'd heard about someone 'getting you' when you started in the mill and my initiation to Kent Mill was one I'd not forget in a hurry. More than 70 years later that prank still makes me chuckle. At the grand old age of 85, it's great to reminisce about the good old days – because, for me, that's precisely what they were. I know a lot of people moan about their time in the mill but I can only reflect fondly on my days there.

Over a 30-year period I worked in and out

of a fair few mills in the Oldham area and I can honestly say now, hand on heart, that I loved every single one of them. And it pains me to think that some of the buildings that produced an industry so important to our country back then no longer exist. The mills I worked in weren't the hellholes they once were, but I think people can't distinguish between the years so it's nice to get the chance to explain what they were really like during my time, starting in 1942. Granted, it was damn hard work, but the people made the mill and I wouldn't have swapped that for the world. If I were young and fit again, I'd go back in tomorrow! But before I explain a bit more about my first job I want to tell you more about me, who I am and how working in the mill came about.

I was born on 18 June 1928 in Oldham, England to William Warrington and Louise (her maiden name was Devall). I had two brothers: Kenneth, who was three years older than me, and Fred, who was five years older. After a mill building boom in the 1860s and 1870s, Oldham overtook Manchester and Bolton in becoming the most productive cotton-spinning town in the world. By 1911 there were over 16 million spindles in the town and by 1928 the number had increased to more than 360 – rectangular brick-built mills, operating night and day.

Mum was a weaver in Newbreck Mill,

Oldham, but Dad, who was from Leicester, worked in the steel industry as a tool turner, someone who made tools. I don't know the finer details but Dad was five years older and they met through my Mum's brother, my uncle William (known simply as Bill), as the two men were friends. But I'm sorry to say I don't know where or when they got married. The only thing I do know is that Mum was in her 40s when I came along. Unlike today, not so many women had babies during what was considered a later age for pregnancy, so I think it's fair to say I was a surprise, especially as she once told me, 'You weren't planned, but you were very welcome.'

When Dad returned from fighting in the royal horse artillery in the First World War, Mum was still in the mill but he struggled to find work. Seemingly, this was a common occurrence for a lot of men. I don't know why he didn't try the mill but I suppose he wanted to do the job he was trained in. So, for a time he did the housework while Mum brought in the wage and then he turned his hand to any odd job, just to bring in some money. But eventually Dad found work, so Mum packed in at the mill and we all uprooted to Leek, a market town in the county of Staffordshire, when I was a baby.

I remember the place we lived as being quite rural and our house was a two up, two down terraced, but I've no idea what the street was called. I just remember I slept in Mum and Dad's bedroom on a camp bed while the two boys were in the back bedroom.

We didn't have much furniture, but I remember an old-fashioned sideboard, which Mum loved, was in the front room, and a couple of chairs; it was all very basic and we didn't have any ornaments.

When I turned five, I started at St Mary's, the convent school. I wore gymslips and blouses for school and other times it was a cotton dress for summer and in winter a jumper or cardigan too. One thing I do remember from this time in my life is feeling happy and loved, and that I laughed a lot. We didn't have much but we weren't the poorest of the poor, if that makes sense. Mum and Dad always made sure we were well fed and clothed – I don't remember ever feeling cold or hungry.

Dad was a bit taller than Mum, with blue-grey eyes (which our Kenneth also had) and light-brown hair. A gentle soul, he didn't drink or smoke and I remember him always being funny and never miserable. Mum was about 5'4", the same height I am now; slim, with brown eyes, which Fred and I inherited. She had brownish hair and wore it short, with a DA at the back and with the front bit flicked up (the DA, 'duck's arse', was a man's style but common for women to copy).

My parents were a loving and a grand couple, who never went out socialising. Always their free time was spent with us, their family. I don't know how much Dad earned but we never went away or to the pictures. Instead, he would take us walking, and whenever I got tired he would pop me on to his shoulders. At night we'd all sit in front of the fire and play card games like snap, or Dad would play with me; he'd be sitting on the chair, I'd go behind him and he'd pull me over his shoulder and tip me upside down, which I loved. I was Mum's little rosebud and Daddy's little cabbage patch.

Mum was a hard worker who was always cooking, cleaning or sewing. She used to buy a bit of material off the market and make us new clothes – all sorts, even trousers; she was really good. Her cooking was delicious too. She always made something out of nothing that would go a long way and was nourishing, such as sausage and mash or stew and dumplings. But my favourite was her potato pie; she made a lovely one with a right big crust on. Breakfast was porridge and, depending on money, it would be made with water or milk, and sometimes I'd put a dollop of jam in. Other times we'd have toast and now and again we'd have cereal, like cornflakes. One thing I never did as a kid was starve, which was evident by my stocky frame. I was short and certainly no skinny kid! One time, when I was at school and about six years old, I wasn't well so Mum took me to the doctor's and he said I was anaemic, so she and I were sent to some medical place and all the mothers there were laughing because I was a right stocky thing.

It was happy days back then and, if I wasn't in the house having fun, I was out on the street, playing with the other kids. I used to knock about with three or four others and our favourite game to play was Whip and Top, which was one of the most popular games back then. A wooden top, it had metal at the bottom and you wound the string around the top of it. As you let it go, it spun around and the idea was to see who could keep the top bit spinning the longest. We also had skipping ropes and played Hopscotch while the boys played marbles, but then we'd all play Cowboys and Indians and swing on the street lamp. We used to throw rope over it and use it like a swing – until we got told off! It was such fun. Sometimes I look at all the toys the kids have today and I'm sure they get fed up with them and still don't have as much fun as we used to.

For example, at Christmas we never got a lot, but Mum and Dad always made sure we had something to open. I remember one year when I was about six I got a doll, which was sat on a swing and you wound it up. I was over the moon as I knew how expensive they were and back then they'd have cost about two shillings, which was a lot then. But at the time Fred, who would have been about 11, was a typical boy who loved pulling things apart and then fixing them back together. And this one day he got hold of my doll and did just that.

'I wanted to see how it works,' he told me, as I walked in to find my dolly in pieces on the table. 'But now I can't put it back together.'

I think I just burst into tears.

'It's OK,' soothed Kenneth.

I was closer to him than to Fred, probably because of the shorter age gap. Each time I tried to play with Fred, he just used to shoo me away, saying, 'I don't want my kid sister following me about!' But Kenneth was like Dad, and he was kind and gentle, and never minded me hanging around him. So, apart from my older brother being a pest, I remember life being just fine. But then tragedy struck our family and it changed things forever.

One day, our Kenneth was rushed to hospital from school.

'Is he poorly?' I asked Mum.

'He's got a poorly mouth,' she replied.

Kenneth had visited the school dentist and somehow his mouth had got infected.

They'd transferred him to hospital and removed some of his teeth to try to catch the infection, but it wasn't working. I can't remember how long he was in hospital for, but the removal of teeth didn't help and the infection spread through his body. He then contracted septicaemia and died when he was just nine years old. At six years old, I didn't really understand or comprehend what had happened, and I know I never went to his funeral. I just remember Kenneth being there one minute, laughing and joking with me, and the next he was gone. I'm not sure exactly when, but, at some point, Mum must have told me the full story.

Apparently, he'd gone to see the school dentist and because he was scared, like most kids are, he kept covering his mouth with his hand. Anyhow, like adults did back then, the dentist gave him a clout around the head and Kenneth fell onto the floor; they believe the germs from the floor got into his mouth. It beggars belief that something like that could have happened, but it did back then. And now, as a parent myself, I can't imagine how Mum and Dad recovered from that. I know they must have put on a brave face for Fred and me as I don't remember them ever being different, but I know this must have been for our benefit.

And, if losing my brother wasn't enough, less than 12 months later, tragedy struck our family for a second time when Dad died of stomach cancer. Dad had suffered with stomach trouble for years, which Mum, to her dying day, believed was due to the gas in the First World War. When he returned from the war, he was, in her words, 'never right'. But, after losing Kenneth, Dad seemed to go downhill. Now, thinking back, I wonder whether the grief of losing his son was too much to bear and he gave up fighting, or it could just have been a cruel coincidence that his cancer had spread. Whatever the reason, by the time he went to get checked out, there was nothing that could be done to save him.

Dad had been in hospital for a while so he asked to come home to die. I remember one day there was a bed in the front room.

'That's for Dad,' said Mum. He never left that bed and she cared for him every hour of every day. I remember one time his friend Bob came to stay for a couple of nights to give Mum a rest. Back then, people believed you could catch cancer, like you can with flu. It's ridiculous even saying that today, but that's what they thought. Anyhow, each time I came home from school I'd go and sit on Dad's bed and tell him all about my day. He mustn't have been eating much as Mum always made sure he had some toffee sweets, and this one time he offered me one.

'Thank you,' I smiled, popping it into my pocket.

'What's up?' he asked.

Like most kids, usually I'd have shoved it straight in my mouth.

'Oh, Mum says I have to wait until I've had my tea,' I replied.

Truth was, Mum told me if Dad ever gave me a sweet I had to give it to her. And because I was a good girl, I did as I was told, but when Mum took it off me I wasn't happy because I wanted to eat it! But I wasn't allowed to. It was still in the wrapper but, because Dad had touched it, Mum wouldn't risk letting me eat it, fearing the worst. I was also told that I was allowed to hug and kiss him but I couldn't have my mouth near his, so was only ever allowed to kiss his cheek.

Dad died when I was seven and again Mum didn't think it was right for me to go to his funeral (children didn't in those days) so a neighbour came and watched me. Afterwards, everyone came back to ours and Mum put a spread on. What happened with Dad was awful and being so young I was a bit mixed up about it all and didn't really know what was happening – especially when Mum announced we were going back to Oldham.

'I have to go work in mill,' she announced one morning.

I knew Mum used to work in the mill and she spoke about it fondly; she didn't mind the work and she liked the people. Mum still had her sisters, Aunt Florence, Aunt Sarah-

Anne and Aunt Lucy, living back in Oldham and of course, with the mills dominating the town and being on most street corners, it was the place for her to find work. And, as an experienced weaver, it was all she knew.

Mum knew someone with a van who kindly transported all our furniture from the old house to our new one while us three caught the train. I might have been born in Oldham but I couldn't remember any of it so, when we moved back, it took a bit of getting used to.

We moved into Spring Street, but I was more used to a rural spot rather than this built-up town with its endless rows of houses and mills everywhere. I didn't like it very much! Our house was two up, two down, with no bathroom and the toilet was at the end of the garden. We had the same furniture as we did in Leek, including the sideboard, in the front room with a couple of chairs. No pictures on the walls, it was all very basic. There was lino flooring with a carpet square and a fireplace which was like a boiler as you lifted the lid and put water in; that was the only source of heating in the house. Mum had a gas cooker in the kitchen, a little table and a flagstone floor, which she used to mop. From the kitchen, wooden stairs led up to two rooms: Fred was in the back room on his own, and I shared the front with Mum.

I started at St Anne's Catholic School in Greenacres, just two minutes away, and, from what I remember, I was quite happy there and enjoyed it. Back then, you stayed at the school until you were 14 so the building was separated between infants and juniors. But, unlike at St Mary's, I wouldn't be able to come home for dinner because Mum wouldn't be there. She had returned to Newbreck Mill, on Huddersfield Road, and, although it wasn't miles away from home, I never questioned why she didn't come back for her dinner. Like I've said, you didn't ask questions then, you just did as you were told. Anyhow, whatever the reason, Mum wasn't coming home for dinner so she'd arranged for me to have school dinners (she had to pay for them at the Education Office).

At the time, I thought this would be fun – until I had them! Our school didn't have a kitchen. It's funny to think now that not all schools then catered for the kids but in those days it was the norm to go home for dinner. Anyhow, because our school didn't serve the dinner, we had to go to a nearby one that did.

So, I remember turning up at this other school about a five- or ten-minute walk away, and me and a bunch of kids waited outside the big kitchen. I hated it! Not only did the other kids, from their dress, look poorer than me but suddenly two women carried out these two big ashcans and started ladling the dinner out of them (an ashcan was what we'd call today a wastebasket or bin that you'd keep outside). Now they may have been brand new and clean, but it looked awful as the two women scooped custard out from them. For me, an ashcan was used to contain the ashes from the fire – not food!

'It's horrid,' I told Mum (I don't think I did three days).

'OK, I'll leave you some money to go buy something,' she replied.

So, from then on, I had chips for dinner, which I bought from the chip shop, and I came home and had them with bread and butter until Mum caught me out and she made me have a sandwich some days instead.

Because Mum started about 7am and wasn't home until after 5pm, I was the last to leave the house and the first to get home; by then Fred had started work. So, the first morning she started back at work, she handed me a key tied to a piece of string.

'Put it around your neck,' she told me. It was the house key.

Mum may have left me in the house but she always made sure she got me up and made me breakfast before she left, and that we were all right.

'Have a good day,' she'd smile, before setting off to the mill.

To help her out, when I got home I'd make sure the kettle was on and tea was in the pot so she could have a brew the moment she came in before she started the tea. I always set the table too. Even though it was tough just being the three of us, we managed. And over tea Mum would regale us with stories of her day.

'Oh, we did have a laugh today,' she'd smirk. 'That Maureen is a joker!'

Mum would tell us how noisy it was in the weaving shed and that it was hard work, but at all times she'd have a smile on her face. But one thing I did notice was her coughing.

'You poorly?' I asked her late one evening.

'No, love,' she replied. 'Just that damn dust from mill getting on my chest.'

Now, at that point, I didn't know much about what Mum did apart from that she weaved. I knew it was hard work, but what fascinated me more was how she talked with fondness of the women in the mill who were her friends. I was still too young to give a thought to what I'd do after I left school, but, with Mum working in the mill and them on most streets, I suppose I always reckoned that's where I'd go. And because she always spoke fondly of them, oddly I wasn't put off. If anything, they sounded like good fun!

I never knew how much money Mum was on, but I knew it wasn't a lot. And I remember when a girl at school once boasted about her Dad's wage: 'He makes £5 a week,' she gushed. Now, at the time we were only kids so we didn't have that much idea of money, but even we knew that was a lot!

Although Mum may not have been earning a lot she always wanted the best for Fred and me. She still sewed all her own clothes and our clothes, too, by hand. And because she worked at the mill, she was allowed to buy material at a cheaper price. Oh, I'll never forget when she made me a velvet dress, I felt so posh!

'It's lovely,' I said, giving Mum a twirl in the kitchen.

One thing about Mum: she always made sure we dressed very well.

Although she worked like a trooper, both in and outside the house, when winter came I always worried about Mum because she'd cough worse than a miner. The minute the temperature dropped and winter took hold, so would Mum's cough. But she just put up with it and did as much as she could before having to call for the doctor. At that age, I didn't realise the severity of her health – but I soon would.

In the meantime, Mum carried on weaving and life carried on turning until war put a spanner in the works.

'Mum, we've been told to carry these everywhere!' I told her when she came home from work one night.

It was 1 September 1939 and our country was at war, so we children had been instructed to carry gas masks with us at all times. They were in a square box with string on to hang over your shoulder and we used to go to school with them – but, thankfully, we never had to use them.

'Yes, you must,' insisted Mum.

'And our teacher said if we forget them then we have to come home and get them,' I added.

'That's right,' she agreed. 'They are important.'

I was 11 years old when war broke out and I was still too young to be worried, but I know Mum was worried for us. And I wasn't surprised; she only had Fred and me now so she wanted us to stay safe. Thankfully, Fred was only just 17 and he was working as a tool turner at Asa Lees in Oldham, but he'd already decided he would volunteer for the Navy when he turned 18. I don't know why he preferred that option to the Army, he just had an interest in the Navy. And two years later he did just that and spent 12 years in the Navy, before coming home, safe and sound.

While the country was adapting to war, I

had more things on my mind: Mum announced we were moving house.

'Where?' I asked.

'To Longfield Street,' she replied. 'It's a nicer house and bit better neighbourhood.'

Mum had been asking our landlord for a while to let her know when another house came up, as ours was damp and not in a great condition. To this day I don't know how she managed it or could afford a better house to rent. I think she may have had some money from Dad's death or she had just saved. Although sad to leave the friends on the street I'd made, I was glad to go.

'When do we leave?' I asked.

CHAPTER TWO

New Beginnings

Longfield Street was like a palace compared to Spring Street. It was at the other end of the town but by far a nicer two up, two down end terrace. Don't get me wrong, the neighbourhood was still poor compared to today's standard, but it was a step up from Spring Street.

'This is nice,' I told Mum. I was on a single bed in the front bedroom with her, while Fred had his own room, but I didn't mind as I knew it wouldn't be forever; my brother was planning on volunteering for the Navy any time soon. Fred and I never got close until I was older, but when he left I still missed him. Not only did he used to do all the repair jobs around the house, but I also just missed him not being around. And, while I missed my friends on Spring Street, it wasn't long before I made new ones. Although we were happy there, it was still wartime and the reality of it seemed to edge closer than we'd dared imagine.

'What's that?' I asked Mum, as we had a peek out the front door at the night sky, careful the air raid warden didn't spot us. The sky was a magnificent, bright red.

'That's Manchester on fire,' she replied, 'where the bombs have hit.'

Oldham was about six miles from Manchester, which sadly, being a major city, was a target for bombs and suffered a lot during the war. They made a heck of a mess of Manchester, especially around the docks.

'Will they hit us?' I asked.

'I'm sure not,' she soothed.

For a time, we only ever seemed to get night sirens but they went off most nights. The warning sound was a level that went up and down; it always went right through me. And then another one, this time the sound on the one level would sound to signal the all clear. We had shelters near us but Mum refused to go in them. The one closest to our house was just a ground-level building with a concrete roof fixed on. It was damp with no lights on, and horrible.

'Well, if something hit that roof and that fell in on us we'd have no chance,' she explained. 'I don't think we're any safer in there than at home.'

Fred agreed, and, obviously, I just went along with what Mum said. The government got local authorities to start issuing huts, steel and round like, which people could put in their garden. They were OK but when it was raining you'd be up to your knees in water so

Mum didn't fancy them either.

So, any time the raid went off, we'd scramble under the kitchen table. Mum thought it was the best place to shield us, especially if the windows shattered. At first, I don't remember feeling scared. If anything, I was willing the raid to go on as long as possible.

'Come on, come on!' I'd say, as Mum just looked and shook her head, as she knew exactly why I was doing it.

'Behave, you,' she'd smile.

You see, if the sirens carried on, or went off after 9pm, we didn't have to go to school the next day as the teachers thought we'd be too tired. But it was funny because, some evenings, it would finish at 8.45pm but you could always guarantee there'd only be half a class the next day because some tried to get away with it.

'Remember, *I* know when the sirens go on and off,' warned the teacher. 'And it was only just after 9pm so you could have come in!'

We could sometimes sit there for hours. Later, when Fred left for the Navy and it was just Mum and me, she'd make a flask and we'd just natter away about all-sorts. I knew Mum was on edge, but she always tried to hide her fear from me and Fred, and especially me when it was just the two of us. When you went to bed, it was hard getting to sleep; you'd be on edge waiting for the sirens to go off, unable to relax, and then, when you did finally fall asleep, they would go off again so Mum would have to come and shake me awake.

'Come on,' she'd say. 'Get up.'

With sleepy eyes and still in my pyjamas, I'd shuffle down the stairs in a zombie state and sit under the table. The only solace was when it dawned on me this probably meant no school the next day. But the older I got, and the more times we had to get under that table, the more concerned I grew. My tummy turned over a bit as I waited to see what would happen. You could hear the planes going over and sometimes even the bombs dropping. They droned and droned, and you thought they were coming down, for sure.

It was terrifying but my mum never showed me she was frightened, although she must have been. She put cushions under the table and said all we can do is keep away from the flying glass. And it got even scarier when we heard about people in Oldham who'd had narrow escapes with the bombs. One woman had an explosion in her garden when she held her wedding reception in her house, but, goodness knows how, no one was hurt.

'It doesn't bear thinking about.' Mum shuddered, but, sadly, that was the reality of war.

And, while the war carried on, so did life. Mum was still at the mill and Fred at Asa Lees, the textile machine manufacturers, so I was still the first person home in the evening. I used to love it when I was about 13 because it meant that I could sit down in peace and read my comic. It was my weekly treat and the day it was being delivered I'd race home from school, full of beans. But no sooner would I be engrossed than Fred would come home and try to snatch it from me.

'I'll have a look at that,' he'd say.

'No, it's mine!' I'd cry, and the rows would start.

He'd always take it off me, the cheeky devil. But he was the man of the house at the time so I couldn't argue with him and, sorry as I was to see him leave home and join the Navy, I did think it was heaven, reading my comic in peace.

It was nice just Mum and me, but it did get tough. We'd head to bed about 9.30pm to 10pm and Mum used to read the magazine *My Weekly* by candlelight to help her get off to sleep. But she'd always have a glass of water beside her bed in case she started coughing – which, sadly, she did.

I'd hear her coughing and coughing, especially in the winter.

'Let me call for the doctor,' I'd say, going into her room to see her.

Her coughing didn't just mean no sleep for her as it woke me too. Once Fred left for the Navy, I'd moved into his room but I could still hear her and when I came into her room she'd be trying to sleep sitting up because lying down just made her coughing worse.

'No, I'm fine,' she'd insist.

Mum just put up with it and carried on rubbing on her Vicks (VapoRub) and trying to do things for herself to stave it off. The doctor was the last resort – it cost to see him – so instead you'd manage as best you could until you had to call him in. Now, I'm not sure what the doctor cost, but you used to pay weekly for what you'd used. And every Friday, I remember a lady would come round and collect, probably the doctor's receptionist. It was so much a week, depending on how many times you'd seen the doctor. But this one time it got so bad I had to have two weeks off school to look after Mum, and eventually the doctor was called and she was diagnosed with bronchitis. Luckily, it wasn't infectious, so we weren't in any danger.

'You have to put this on her skin, where her lungs are,' explained the doctor, handing me a tin of kaolin poultice, a thick, liquid-like putty. 'It should help, but the best thing for it is to give up the mill.'

I had to stand the kaolin in a tin of hot water for it to soften and then get a knife and spread it onto her upper back. It was so thick and gloopy, like spreading treacle, but I didn't care as long as it made her better. I had to stay off school a week or two every year to care for Mum and thankfully the school didn't seem to mind.

Although she got better in time, especially once the winter chill dispersed, Mum knew she couldn't carry on like this and would have to quit. Eventually, she did. I can remember I was still at school but I didn't have long to go before I finished. And I know she didn't want to leave; she was sad to leave the people and the money. Mum hated having to ask for handouts too. Back then, benefits weren't what they are today, although there were some.

I would do all the cooking, cleaning and shopping. Mum was more upset than anything else because I had to do it, but I didn't mind. Our radio was powered via an accumulator so I'd go to the shop to get a fully charged one so she could listen to it, and in the evening we'd listen to Billy Cotton and his band, Wakey Wakey. I'd dance about the living room and Mum would just nod her head along and smile: she loved to watch me dance, although she couldn't do it herself because after Dad died she never went out to dances.

And whenever Mum got worried about money I'd reassure her: 'We'll manage, and

I'll be working soon.' I didn't begrudge looking after her but it did mean that I had to grow up and learn fast, probably far more than I imagine a 13- or 14-year-old would today. Mum had shown me the odd thing and obviously I watched her in the kitchen but, with rations, cooking proved a challenge and I had to learn fast. Soon I was cooking stews and pies – not that I could make Mum's potato pie as well as she could, though.

I found out from a neighbour that I had to melt the butter and add a bit of milk to it, and set it again to make it last longer. We were only allowed 2oz for a week and, well, if you think that you can use that in two days now, you can imagine how little it was. At school I did cookery classes so I was also taught how to make sugarless, fatless cakes by using saccharin and liquid paraffin in place of butter and fat. I dissolved the artificial sweetener into a glass of water and added a tablespoon of liquid paraffin to the flour. It actually tasted all right once it was cut open and I'd added jam; Mum thought it was great.

Other food rationed was meat, as well as all dairy foods but we didn't do too bad for milk. We got 4oz of meat, the odd chop or mincemeat and then 2oz of corned beef for sandwiches or to fry it in batter. Corned beef fritters, all sorts of ideas came out. The bread wasn't white – it was almost black and looked awful! I'm not sure what they used to replace it with, but it was something to do with the flour to make it last longer (everyone was glad when the war was over so we could have white bread again!). And because trade halted we couldn't get oranges, lemons or bananas.

But while I was more than happy to help around the house, when I reached the age of 14, work was on my mind. And, despite seeing Mum suffer from the mill, it still didn't put me off. When a school friend of my mum's offered to show me around the mill – to give me an idea of what it would be like, so I could decide for myself if it was for me – I jumped at the chance.

One Saturday morning, I met her at this particular mill. The woman, Olive, was nice and from a good family – and not like the rest of the women in there! She took me into the ring room, for the ring spinning, where there were two rows of machines with cops (a corn-shaped object that holds the cotton) and you put them on and set the machines going. But, as the other women filtered in, I couldn't believe how rough some of them were. Not in a nasty way, just a bit rough around the edges in the sense that you could see some of them hadn't combed their hair for a day or two, and the language they used was very colourful.

'Aye, you'll have to think twice before you come in here!' they laughed.

But I didn't feel intimidated; they were all very welcoming. I was just a little shocked by their behaviour and what was going to come next – especially when I went to the toilet with the woman who'd brought me so she could have a ciggie. The girls in there who were smoking were swearing away like it was normal, and, if I wasn't shocked enough then, I was when I saw all the naughty rhymes and slogans on the toilet wall.

'Oh my goodness!' I gasped, reading one, which said:

When you enter these marble halls,
please use the paper and not the walls,
for it is a dirty trick to wipe your arse on a
*   brick!*

'Don't be reading that!' my friend laughed. 'Your mum'll kill ya!'

My friend took me to a few other departments in the mill so I could get a feel for the place and, even though it was noisy and hot, I loved it.

'How did you get on?' Mum asked when I got home.

'Well, I like it but I don't want to work in that department,' I replied. 'The women swear a lot.'

As I explained to Mum all that I'd seen and heard, she just smiled and said, 'Yes, I do know about that – I'd rather you didn't go in that department.'

To be honest, Mum didn't want me to go in the mill at all. It wasn't that she thought I could do better, as she had enjoyed her time in there, she was just desperately worried I'd end up the same as her with the awful bad chest. And she was in so much agony with it, she didn't want me to go through the same thing.

But as my days got closer to leaving school in July 1942, I had to make a decision. My mind was already swayed towards the mill, as, to be quite honest, that was the major source of employment anyhow and I don't even know what else I'd have done, but then my friend Joan confirmed it for me.

'Oh, come on, we'll have some fun!' she said.

I was friendly with Joan and her sister Iris, who was a year or two older and already working in the mill. The minute she said that, I was sold! After all, I wanted to go with my mates and have fun, and even Mum admitted she had had a good time in there, so it made sense.

'OK, but give it three month and, if your chest starts playing up, you're coming out,' Mum reasoned, when I told her I was going to try to get in mill.

'Agreed,' I smiled.

So, on the Friday, my last day at school, someone from the Education Office visited us and asked what job we wanted to do.

'Work in mill,' I replied.

One of the girls said shop work, but Joan and me just smirked at each other – we weren't going to do that.

'I'm not working *all* day on a Saturday,' Joan said. 'With mill, you finish at 12pm, but she'll have to work till 8pm!'

It's funny, thinking back now, how your brain works when you are that age. Anyhow, once I'd said the mill, this man wrote something down on a card and handed it to me.

'Go to Kent Mill on Monday and head to the office and the manager will be expecting you,' he said. 'You'll be trained as a winder.'

I knew Mum's job was down in the weaving shed, where it was noisiest – she ran looms to weave cloth – so I also knew a winder was in the winding room and they wound thread onto the spindles used in shuttles.

'Thank you,' I replied.

You didn't get a choice of mill so I never gave it a second thought that Joan and me might not work in the same one. When we looked at each other's cards, we were disappointed to see that she had been given the Newroyd Mill in Waterhead, Oldham.

'Oh, mine is miles away,' I said.

'Mine is closer and I think it's only a small one,' she replied. 'But I know a few are going to yours.'

But it didn't matter; we were both excited to start work regardless, and anyhow I knew I'd see her every weekend. That night I went home and told Mum the good news, but I didn't get the reaction I was hoping for.

'It's damp and hard work,' she said.

While I was disappointed, I knew she was only concerned for my health and didn't want the dust affecting me as badly as it had her.

'I'll be OK, Mum,' I pleaded. 'There are three from our class going to same mill, so it will be good.'

And so began the same argument...

'Right, you can go,' she said. 'But I'll give you about three month and, if you start becoming ill, you're out! Are we agreed?'

'Yes,' I cheered.

I don't think either of us thought I'd end up staying over 30 years.

So, by the time Monday morning rolled around, I couldn't wait to get started. Kent Mill was in Chadderton, near Oldham, so a good bus ride away. I'd been told to wear a cotton overall, so I think I actually bought that instead of Mum making it. By now, Mum was getting older and her chest was worse, so her days of sewing were, sadly, behind her. It had a square neck and a little belt that tied at the back. Underneath I wore a cotton dress because Mum had warned me not to wear anything too warm because it would get hot.

On my first day, Mum handed me a case with my dinner in and I proudly walked to the bus stop, feeling all grown up. But because I wasn't very tall, when I sat down on the seat my feet didn't even touch the floor, so when I asked the conductor for a return ticket because I was starting work, he just smirked and said, 'If you can't touch the floor, you won't be going to work!'

Soon, the bus pulled up and I jumped off. I walked down this slip road and, suddenly, the big, long mill came into view. All red brick, it had five floors and looked as long as my street.

'My goodness!' I gulped.

But despite the size I wasn't put off and the knots in my stomach were more excitement than nerves; I just couldn't wait. And, when I walked through the railings and inside, it seemed quite tidy and better maintained than the mill I'd been shown around; there didn't seem to be as much dust in the air either.

My instructions were to head to the office (which they called 'the cabin') to meet the boss, who would then put me with someone to show me the ropes.

'Hello,' I said timidly, passing him my card.

'Ah yes, we were expecting you today,' said the manager.

Tall and slim, he was very nice but to me, of course, he was old. He told me my hours were 7am to 5pm, with an hour for lunch at 12pm and a 10-minute brew break in the morning; Saturday mornings would be 7am to 12pm and, while training, I'd start on two shillings and sixpence, which wasn't too bad, but, once I was running my own frame, I'd go on piece work so could make my own wage. After explaining, he asked me to follow him into the winding room.

The room was huge with whitewashed walls and very light. I followed him down the main alley (known as 'the path') past the machines, which had these huge straps at the end of each one. It was also very noisy in there.

'I thought you could be taught by some-one you know,' he explained.

'Hello, Doris,' the woman in front of me smiled.

She was my neighbour, Eileen, and lived just a few doors up from me. I'd told her I was starting so I'm not sure if she'd sug-gested she should train me or whether the carder (the manager of that department) had asked her, but either way it was a relief to know I was with someone nice and some-one I already knew.

I knew a couple of other girls from school were also starting that day, as winders, but they were in a different part of the room from me. I'd seen them outside and, like me, they were excited but, unlike me, they hadn't been nosey and already gone into a mill for a snoop about. And I hadn't been put off by the horror stories; the only thing I'd heard was about a girl from school called Annie who was hit in the eye by a metal claw, which snapped off the straps running the machinery. Now she had partial sight in one eye and had had to leave the mill. But stories like that didn't put me off for I knew accidents could happen in any walk of life and, as far as I was concerned, after losing my brother and dad, it seemed worse things happened *outside* the mill.

I stood beside my neighbour in front of this long frame. She explained that each winder works on about a third of it. I couldn't tell you how long each frame was but it was a heck of a length! She told me to put the weft (thread) on a little spindle, wrap it around, fasten it through and then I was to set it off until it ran out and keep putting new cones of thread on. So, you had to stand there and keep watching for when it got full. Because of the noise she had to shout and use her hands a bit. Suddenly, it hit me how loud it must have been for Mum, as *this* was bad enough!

I knew Mum had learned to lip read in the

weaving shed because that was essential, but she also did what they call 'mee-mawing', which is a kind of miming language, and that's why I soon picked up that people used it in there. So, for example, if someone wanted you to watch their machines they'd say, 'Keep your eye (touching their eye) on my (touch their chest) frame (touch the frame) while I go for a smoke (do smoking sign).'

Suddenly, it was 12pm and time for dinner.

'You've done well so far,' smiled my neighbour.

I met up with the other girls from school and, as it was summer, we sat out on the fire escape eating our sandwiches.

'It's good, isn't it?' I said.

'Yes, but noisy,' replied one.

'And I'm glad for a sit down now,' sighed the other.

That was true, and even though I'd only been in there a few hours already I knew it was going to be hard work, standing all the time. But I felt proud of myself doing my first day at work and I couldn't wait to tell Mum all about it.

'It was great!' I gushed. 'Everyone is really nice and it's clean and tidier than I thought.'

'Oh, that's good,' said Mum. And she was even more pleased when I told her our neighbour was training me. 'Well, at least I know someone's got an eye on you,' she smirked. 'And how's that chest?'

'Fine!' I laughed.

To be honest, the only thing that was worrying me at this point was the distance to the mill. It was a good half-hour on the bus, which made the day that bit longer and more tiring, but, for now, I was keeping schtum as I didn't want to leave.

By the end of my first weekend, I was dying to meet up with Joan and, on Saturday night, our school had arranged some social events. Although the picture houses were open, it was safer to go where more people were and so the school, even though we were no longer pupils, had arranged for social evenings for us. We played table tennis, or put records on and danced, and, because the teachers were present, Mum felt that bit happier about me going.

'Make sure you take your gas mask,' she said. They also had shelters at school, as they'd dug down in the playground so, if a siren was to go off, Mum knew I'd be safe. 'And you know your way home?'

With no street lights permitted to be switched on in the streets, they were pitch black, so you had to remember your way home if ever you went anywhere at night.

'Of course,' I reassured her.

'OK, but do be careful,' she fretted.

Mum was so lovely. Even though I knew she was worried and she'd have preferred me to stay at home, she never once stopped me from going out. And I remember that winter we had bad snow and she must have been worried sick, what with that and the sirens, but still she didn't stop me.

'I'll be fine,' I insisted.

Anyhow, this one time in winter, I plodded on down the street by myself. At the time, we had leg tan on as we couldn't get nylons or stockings, unless you went out with the Yanks, but I was far too young for any of that carry-on, so I had a seam drawn on up the back of my leg. I was off to the dance and no sooner had I turned the corner of my street than I fell. All the stuff came off my legs and I dread to think what I must have looked like. Really I should have gone back but I didn't want to miss the dance, so I just carried on.

We had once been able to carry torches but as soon as the night raids started they were banned. They were so strict and they'd have the ARP (Air Raid Precaution) air warden patrolling the streets and, if there was a chink of light peeking out from your blackout curtain, you were in for it! They'd knock on your door and order, 'Get that bloody light out!'

I loved the mill and, before I knew it, three

weeks had passed by, so I was made up when, a few weeks in, the nice boss man came over and asked my neighbour, 'Is she ready now?'

'Yes, I'm sure she is,' she told him.

So, I was put on a frame close to her.

'OK?' she asked.

'Yes,' I nodded, a bundle of nerves and excitement.

But I just got on with it and, to be honest, found it fine. And once I was doing the proper job and not training, my wage went up to two shillings and sixpence a week – that would be about 25 pence today.

'Wow!' I gushed, knowing this would help Mum out no end (I used to give her my wage and she'd give me a bit back).

When I was about 15, after being at the mill for over a year, Joan asked me to go to a dance hall one night, away from the school, as her sister Iris was going.

'Can I go, please?' I asked Mum.

'As long as you're careful and you stay with Iris,' she replied.

Mum wasn't strict and she never stopped me from going out. She trusted me that I wouldn't do anything silly, although there were one or two places she banned me from going because she didn't approve of what went on there with the drinking.

Soon Joan and I were going to dances in the town. Being wartime, there were a lot of

Yanks at them, trying to win the hearts of the local ladies. They had plenty of money, and would give out chewing gum and nylon, so of course the women fell at their feet! Our lads at the dances used to say they were 'over-dressed, overpaid and over here' as I'm guessing they didn't like it. I knew a few girls who fell for a Yank and ended up pregnant, so at the end of the war they had to move back home with them. In fact, the Yank soldiers had to ask the permission of their captain if they could marry an English girl. But all that nonsense wasn't for me and I was far too young to dance with one, never mind be swept off my feet! In fact, the thought of going with a man made me rigid with fear. I knew nothing about the birds and the bees and, up to this point, had never had a proper boyfriend.

Anyhow, each time I'd been to a dance hall, the next day or the Monday at work, I'd sit with the other girls and talk about it. One time, I'd gone to the dance hall Mother had told me not to.

'There is this pub around the corner and it doesn't matter what age you are, they'll still serve you,' I told the girls in work. There was a little gang of us who sat around having dinner together.

'*No!*' they gasped.

'Oh yes!' I said. 'Some girls my age came in to dance *half-drunk!*'

Now, I had gone to this dance hall but, because I had to be home for 9pm, I'd never seen the women come in drunk, it was just what Joan had told me happened.

Anyhow, one Saturday afternoon not long after, I was walking through town with Mum when a girl from our gang at the mill stopped to say hello. As we got chatting, all of a sudden she said to Mum, 'Do you know that dance hall Doris goes to? Well, it's not a fit place.'

Stunned, I couldn't believe she was about to tell on me about the dance hall Mum had barred me from.

'You shouldn't be mixing with them,' she added. 'You shouldn't be going there as it's not a nice place.'

This girl was a little bit older than me, and I know she was worried but I was shocked she'd told my mum.

'I was with Joan and we didn't see anything like that as we'd already left,' I protested, defending myself as I knew Mum wouldn't be at all happy. 'Honestly, Mum, you know I'm home for 9pm.'

As we bid our goodbye and walked on, Mum knew I was telling the truth.

'I know, but that's why I don't want you to go,' she said. 'So, I'd rather you just go to the other two.'

'OK, I will,' I said. And I stuck to my word.

CHAPTER THREE

Love of the Mill

Soon, I didn't think twice about getting up at 6am to go to work; it just became a normal part of what I did, like eating or brushing my teeth. I loved the mill – or, more accurately, the people in the mill. The way I saw it, I got to get out of the house, which made a nice change, and spend the day with friends. I'd settled in well with the girls I worked with, and there was a real mix of us, from school leavers, teenagers, married and older, but their age or background didn't matter as we all got on so well. And when we stopped the machines for dinner we'd all sit around chatting about anything from the weekend: boys, films and fashion. But, while we tried to keep our spirits high and carry on as normal, none of us had forgotten that we were still at war.

I was supposed to carry my gas mask to work, but to be honest I don't think I always did. It's odd living in wartime as you just get on with it, and after a while hearing the sirens or not having certain foods to eat becomes the norm. But what never became easier to swallow was seeing the look of worry and anxiety across the faces of those women who had sons and husbands fighting in the war. Although we tried to have a laugh, we had to be sensitive to their needs, and when one of them wasn't in work then you knew it was bad news.

'Is Janet not in today?' asked one of the older women.

'No,' replied one. 'She got a telegram about her son. It doesn't look good.'

Women would receive telegrams that informed them their loved one may have been injured, taken as a prisoner of war or even killed, and you knew it was bad if you didn't see them for a few days – or even longer.

The mood in the mill could get sombre and it was just awful when we heard someone in there had been directly affected. And I remember our neighbour's daughter lost her husband. He was killed in Japan, and I don't know how old he was but she was only 19.

'My mother says her mum said she's not moved off her sofa for two days,' I told the women.

'That's awful,' they gasped. 'So sad and so very young to be a widow.'

Our mill was predominantly women as all the men were abroad, but the few men that worked there were either too old to fight or had been excused on the grounds of ill health. But whatever the reason they never spoke about not being called up and we never asked. I suppose some of them were secretly relieved, but others must have felt guilty and ashamed that they couldn't do their duty, their bit. A lot of them went to work as air raid wardens to help out.

I was relieved in a way not to be married and not to have the constant worry. Of course, I was concerned about Fred being in the Navy, and I knew Mum was worried sick, so when he came home on leave, on 2 September 1945, just before the war was declared over, it was the best news ever.

'We have to head to the Town Hall,' insisted Fred. 'Everyone is outside celebrating.'

By now, he was courting a nice girl called Alice, so the three of us went up there. I was 17 and Alice was a year or two older. Mum didn't mind me going with them and she was happy enough to stay indoors and listen to the news on the wireless. Anyway, because Fred was wearing his sailor suit, and I knew he had a spare one, I had the crazy idea as a bit of fun to wear his spare one. And, aye, it fitted me like a glove and, if I do say so myself, I didn't look half bad! To finish off the look, I tied my hair up and popped on his hat.

'Let's go!' I cheered, as the three of us linked arms, with Alice in the middle. And as we approached the celebrations some lads passed us by and shouted to Alice, 'You're a greedy devil, aren't you?' thinking I was a lad. We did have some laughs that night, it was great fun.

The next day in the mill, everyone went crackers, rejoicing at the news. I know there was still a lot up in the air, like rationing continuing and people waiting for their loved ones to return home, but it felt like we could breathe again – and it was as though the mill somehow sensed the relief, too.

Up until then, the mill had been a good laugh – well, in my eyes, anyway – but, by 'eck, I hadn't known the half of it! Suddenly you could feel the atmosphere in the place change almost overnight. The tense feeling the war had created was lifted and now the place became even more fun and full of pranks.

'Fancy helping us out later?' asked one of the girls near to me. 'We're going to play a trick on the lads.'

'Ooh, yes!' I giggled mischievously. Although, really, I was quite willing just to watch what was happening and not get involved, I knew I'd have no option but to be dragged in.

The gents' toilets were at one end of the room and the women's at the other. The men who worked in the mill wore overalls with braces on, so they used to leave them in the toilet lockers and change into them first thing, and back out of them at night. So, once all the men had gone into the toilets at 5pm to change out of their overalls, ready for home, we all snuck into the room next to them and hid.

'What happens now?' I whispered.

'You'll see!' sniggered one, holding up a piece of rope. And with the count of three, one said, 'Now!' With that, all the girls – including me, a little behind being on cue – leapt out and, quick as you like, started to tie the rope across the male door so they couldn't get out! As we erupted into giggles, it wasn't long before we heard the men trying the door from inside and cursing us.

I wasn't sure how long the charade was going to go on, and, believe me, I wanted to stay longer, but I had to get home.

'Eh, I don't know about you but I've a bus to catch,' I said, slipping away.

The next day, I couldn't wait to get in and hear what had happened. And it wasn't long before one of the girls saw me walking in and told me that they'd kept them in for a while before they eventually untied the knot.

'But then we had to hide,' she laughed. 'I'm still not sure if they know who did it, but I reckon they have a good idea – so watch your back!'

As the men came out, they were heard

saying, 'They're at it again, the devils. Who is it this time?' But in fairness they took it well and had a laugh about it, and it wasn't long before a couple of them were over, quizzing me.

'Wurr you one of 'em?' asked one of the men.

'Course not!' I sniggered.

'Aye, I believe that,' he smirked. 'Nowt but trouble, you lot!'

I knew he was kidding and they thought it was funny, though. But to be sure, I was careful never to go in the loos after 5pm in case they got me back.

There were all different characters in the mill and, while most of us got on and had a bit of a laugh together, some kept themselves to themselves. There was one woman in our bit who hardly left her machine so we nick-named her 'Mrs Piss Quick'. Older than me, she was probably married and would speak when spoken to but otherwise she was quiet and kept herself to herself, always going home at lunchtime. But among the majority of women there was always good banter and humour flying around – especially from the older women to the younger girls, who they'd tease about life.

Like today, back then, love made the world go around, and, even though we were far more innocent than girls today, it still didn't stop this from being the main topic of conversation in the mill. If someone heard that one of the girls had been to the pictures with a boy, they'd get a grilling from the older ones at dinner the next day.

'Well, go on, tell us,' they'd prompt. 'Was he a good kisser, or what?'

The poor girl in question would go as bright as a beetroot, while the rest fell about laughing, but it was all harmless and not at all nasty. But we were so innocent back then; I knew nothing of the birds and the bees. My mum certainly didn't tell me anything and I was too shy to ask, and, even when I listened to the dirty jokes the older women told, I still didn't have a clue.

'You better cover your ears for this one!' they'd tease.

My friends and me weren't open about sex as people are today, and we'd never have dreamt of asking each other what we knew. So, the minute a girl got engaged or married, I'd stand there in shock as the other young girls fired questions at her.

'What's *it* like?' asked one.

'How do you know what to do?' quizzed another.

But, sadly, the girl in question would never reveal anything.

'Don't be so nosey. Find out for yourself,' she'd reply.

Up until then, I'd not had any serious boy-friends but, one day in the mill, when my friend Lillian and me spotted a new guy on the floor fixing some pipes, she gave me a nudge in the right direction.

'He's new,' she said. 'Looks al'reet.'

As we walked past him, we gave him some banter about something or other silly, and soon Lillian found out he was a plumber, just there to do a bit of work.

'He's got his eye on you,' she added. 'He's called Jack and they want to double-date us at the pictures.'

Lillian was courting a boy from the mill called Frank and this plumber had got friendly with him, it seemed.

'Oh right,' I replied.

And later that day Jack sauntered over to my machine to ask me out. Tall and good-looking, he was 18 like me and seemed a nice lad, so I agreed. Back home after work, I told Mum I was going out with a man who'd been at the mill.

I put on my best dress and coat, and my hair was in a wave and up in a sweep at the front; the sides were curled up, held there by grips. Mum didn't like the idea of make-up, so at the time I didn't wear any but, when I told her Lillian was wearing some, I asked her if I could, too.

'Well, you can, but I don't want you going looking like a painted doll,' she warned.

'Just wear a touch – you don't need any as you have plenty of colour already.'

So, I put on a touch of face powder and wore a pale-red lipstick, which I'd borrowed from Lillian. Not sure where she'd got it from but I knew she had an older sister so it may have been hers.

'Don't be late home,' said Mum. 'And just be careful!'

Lillian and me met them both at the picture house on Park Lane in Oldham, which, like a lot of picture houses from back then, is no longer there and we watched a Bill Cosby Western. I felt a little nervous when Jack walked me home and grabbed my hand, and then when we said goodnight on the doorstep he leaned in to give me a kiss (just a peck) on the lips. Well, even that was a lot for me! Not only was I too frightened to go any further, I didn't know what further meant then.

The next day at work, Lillian and I chatted about our date and soon the other women joined in.

'Was he all right? Was he a good kisser?' they asked. 'Did he take you right home?'

'Yeah, course he did,' I replied, my cheeks turning crimson.

After that, I started courting Jack and would see him once during the week and every weekend. If we didn't go to each other's house, we'd go for a walk, to the pictures or to the dance halls. Sometimes we double-dated with Lillian and Frank and other times we were on our own. But, while Lillian told me she was in love with Frank, and went on to marry him, I never felt quite the same about Jack.

'He's talked about getting engaged but I'm not sure,' I'd admitted to Lillian. I liked Jack but he could sometimes be a bit jealous and I was starting to question our future.

'I wouldn't stick him two minutes!' said Alice, who was now my sister-in-law after she'd married Fred. She and Fred were living at home with Mum and me until they found a place to live. 'Always asking where have you been, who've you been with? Just think about it!'

She was right, so I started to try to cool things off. When he asked me out one Friday night, I told him I was staying in to wash my hair – a saying that has now become popular but which, back then, was actually genuine and not used as a brush-off! It was a Friday ritual to wash your hair on bath night, as you only washed it once a week, and then I'd put curlers in it, ready for the weekend. Anyhow, he wasn't happy, especially when I ended up going to the fair with Alice and he found out. We had a bit of a spat and I told him I wanted to end it. I wasn't a bit bothered and soon I was out dancing again, learning to Waltz,

Tango and Quickstep, or I was off out into Manchester with Joan and her sister Iris to have a look around the shops and, if we could afford it, buy a blouse.

And the girls at work weren't upset to hear the news, which made me feel better about what I'd done.

'Have you packed him in?' they asked.

'Yes,' I replied.

'I always thought he was an awkward bugger,' said one.

I loved the women in there. They were so real and genuine, and also some of the strongest women I ever met. But they had to be, as they were working full-time, running a home and being a wife and mother. I know women do the same today but they had it far tougher then. And, although I was happy enough in Kent Mill, when Alice suggested I went to her mill, it got me thinking perhaps a change would be good.

'Why don't you come with us?' suggested Alice one tea-time. 'I'm sure it's more money.'

She worked in the card room at the Wye Mill, which was in Crompton, an industrial town three miles from Oldham. There was actually Wye Mill No. 1, which was built in 1914, and then built opposite in 1925 was Wye Mill No. 2. Both these great big mills were demolished in 1974, and I believe there are now houses in their place.

'Well, I do like that room,' I replied.

I'd been shown round the card room (a huge room with loads of windows, but lots of dust) by the family friend who'd taken me to the mill that day when I was still at school; I loved it at Kent Mill but I was ready for a change and I needed to bring in more money for me and Mum. She'd never asked me, I just knew we needed it. Besides it was a trek to Kent Mill and, although this one was still a bus ride away, it was a change of scenery.

'Well, come and see the boss,' she added.

I was sad to leave Kent Mill and all the people, and everyone was lovely to me when I told them. But before I knew it, I'd soon settled into Wye Mill.

I didn't work alongside Alice but I was on the ground floor and the card room was noisy and dusty, yet it still didn't put me off. Unlike in the Kent Mill, I didn't see the main boss of the mill but I was told to report to my immediate boss, the carder. He was responsible for the card room and then he had one or two under carders and my job was a card tenter, which meant I was to look after or tend to a card machine: I had to separate and assemble the cotton to make it easier to spin.

I worked on a machine that was taller than me. With one main roller and smaller ones surrounding it, the rollers turned round and you brought the cotton through each one until it tightened up. By the end, you had a large rope made of fibres. I soon got the hang of them and loved the work. And, although it was a different mill, the conditions were the same. By now I was 19, and, although the Saturday-morning working had stopped, nothing else was any different, really – especially not the banter!

There was the usual ribbing, and, of course, whenever I went out at the weekend to the dance halls with Joan, the women always wanted to know the gossip of a Monday dinnertime.

'So, any men?' they'd ask.

Usually, I'd say no. Since Jack, I hadn't been fussed, but on this occasion, in 1947, it was different.

'I did, actually,' I replied.

'Ooh,' they swooned. 'Well, come *on!*'

Jim Cook was 21, but unlike me he couldn't dance so he and his mates used to just sit there and watch. I'd seen him a few times. He was a tall, good-looking lad, with brown eyes, but I'd never spoken to him. Anyhow, this one Saturday night, he approached me and asked if I'd like to write to him. He was on leave from the Army but stationed somewhere in Greece.

'So, you going to write then?' asked one of the women.

'Yes, I think I will,' I said.

But a few weeks later I felt disappointed when I hadn't heard back, even after writing a couple more times, especially when the women at work kept quizzing me.

'Any news from Army boy?' they'd ask.

'No, have I 'eck!' I replied, shaking my head.

'Well, what's he playing at?' they wanted to know.

'I don't know and I don't care,' I replied. 'I'm fed up of him and I've had enough!'

'Oh, well, don't worry, love,' they soothed. 'Plenty more where he came from!'

But a few weeks later I was walking around the town when I bumped into him.

'Why didn't you write?' he asked.

'I did – a few times,' I replied.

'Well, I never received them,' he said.

I believed him, so we went for a cup of tea, and when he asked me out I said yes.

But Mum was none too pleased when I told her Jim had taken me to a pub.

'As long as you don't drink a lot,' she said.

'I don't,' I told her.

In fact, I don't think I drank at all as I didn't like it. The only drink I remember liking was Babycham, but that was a few years later.

Mum called him a 'rough diamond' but she didn't mind him, and months later, when he proposed, she was pleased. Although I was happy, I was also worried about Mum if I moved out of the family house.

By then, her health was bad and she struggled awfully with her chest. I had to go in many a night when I heard her coughing so I knew she wasn't fit to be left alone, especially as Fred and Alice, being married, had their own place.

'It's fine, we can live there for a while until we get a house,' Jim told me.

On cloud nine, I couldn't wait to get in the mill and show off my ring.

'Ooh, lovely!' cooed the women, as I held out my left hand, proudly showing off my plain gold ring.

'We're so happy for you,' they gushed.

And I knew they were. That was the thing about the mill, there was such great camaraderie and everyone looked out for one another and wished them well.

Within 12 months of our meeting, the date was set for our wedding. I'd arranged to have a week off work afterwards but I worked right up to my big day. My wedding was on the Saturday so I was in work on the Friday and so touched by all the presents people gave me. During the celebrations in the mill, someone pulled out this chamber pot, what they would use as a toilet in the night, and they poured beer and ginger biscuits into it. They handed it to me and I had to take a sip and walk around the room, giving everyone else a sip. So funny, yet it looked ruddy awful! It was such a laugh and I couldn't believe how much effort everyone had made.

And as I was leaving work, everyone was wishing me well.

'See you tomorrow,' said some, as I'd invited them to the day do and more to the evening do. Usually, everyone was out the door at 5pm but tonight they seemed to be hanging around, waiting for me to put on my grey woollen, double-breasted coat. And, as I pulled it on, I suddenly realised why: they'd only gone and filled the arms with bobbins and sewed the ends of the sleeves up!

'Brilliant!' I cried.

As the workers fell about laughing, they all stood and watched me walk to the bus stop like that. And to this day, I dread to think what the bus driver and the other passengers must have made of it. They'd well and truly sent me off in a good style!

That evening, I had a bath and washed my hair, then just stayed in with Mum. I remember telling Mum I was nervous about the wedding – and the wedding night itself. Like I said, I had no idea so she tried to explain a little.

'You have to do whatever he says,' she said. 'It won't be very easy, but you'll get used to it in time.'

And the next day, on 11 December 1948, we married at St Anne's Catholic Church in Oldham. Fred gave me away and I wore a bridal gown and veil, which I'd borrowed off Alice, and carried a beautiful bouquet with a white ribbon and had two bridesmaids. One was Jim's sister, who wore a pink dress that was the new length, halfway between knee and ankle, and the other was a neighbour's little girl.

We had our reception in a function room next door to the ballroom where I used to go, called Hills Stores. It was a big reception with about 50 people there, including many from the mill, and that night we had a do in The Black Horse pub. Back then, it was the thing to have it in different venues, unlike today.

Anyhow, because I hadn't a clue about the wedding night, when my new husband and me returned home and went to bed, there was I rooting for my nightie, which I couldn't find. I later found out that Fred and his mates had gone in and shifted my nightie and Jim's pyjamas, then thrown them into the big zinc bath on the shelf in the kitchen. So, I managed to find an old pair of pyjamas to wear until my husband told me to take them off! Now, there are some details a lady must keep to herself.

Jim and me had moved into the back

bedroom and it was lovely having a week off work. We couldn't afford to go away anywhere, so instead we just had day trips out to Blackpool and Southport. But, before I knew it, it was time to return to the mill – this time as a married lady.

As expected, I had my leg pulled a bit as I got teased over the wedding night, and, when the younger ones started firing questions at me, I just replied with: 'You'll have to find out like I had to do!'

But I didn't mind being back, especially that time of year. There was a good atmosphere in the run-up to Christmas. The mills never had a tree as it was too dangerous because of the machinery and the few trimmings that were up had to remain close to the windows. Up to this point, I don't ever remember a mill Christmas party, but there was always something going on.

I remember in my first mill, when I was just 15, the women asked me to go for a meal with them after work one night. Mum said I was allowed to go and then when they all trotted off to the pub for a drink one of the older women, who didn't like that sort of thing, walked me home.

On Christmas Eve, people would nip over to the pub for a drink or two. Back in the day, they would return to their machines a little tipsy but that was soon stamped out and instead we started to have our own get-together near our machines. We'd wear silly hats, bring in some sandwiches and have a singsong.

And now, as one of the workers ran past me, chasing one of the few male workers while holding a piece of mistletoe, I couldn't help but laugh.

'What's she doing?' I asked the woman beside me.

'Getting a kiss,' she smiled. 'They have to pay 50 pence if they're caught and she kisses them, but if you go after a boss they have to pay £1. But they can only be chased once.'

As laughter filled the air, it was things like this that made the mill special. I mean, where else could you have just good, honest fun? And at that moment in time I was more than happy to spend my next 40 years there until my retirement. It was just a shame it never ended up that way, and as everyone laughed and joked no one could possibly have known what lay ahead.

CHAPTER FOUR

End of an Era

After two years of being married, I was delighted to announce more good news to my friends in the mill.

'I'm pregnant!' I cried.

'Oh, that's great news, love,' they told me.

And, as my belly grew, I was getting more excited.

'You'll not get close enough to that machine soon!' joked some of the male workers.

'I'm more sick of this heat!' I gasped, wiping my brow. It was hot in the card room, but as it was July and I was eight months pregnant it was 10 times worse than normal, so it was the only time I'd been relieved to leave the mill. At the time, maternity allowance was only six weeks before and seven after the birth (or you could swap them around).

And a week over my due date, on 11 August 1950, our daughter Lynda was finally born at the Royal Hospital, in Oldham.

'She must have liked it in there!' joked Mum.

It was great being at home with Lynda, and seven weeks later it was hard having to return to the mill and leaving her with Mum. But I had no choice as we needed the work: Jim was a driver and my £6-a-week wage (I was on piece work) was needed.

'She'll be OK,' soothed Mum. 'And you'll enjoy it when you go back.'

Of course, she was right, but it was still tough leaving Lynda. Already I'd nipped into the mill to show her off and I knew it would be nice to see everyone again – I just wish we'd been entitled to more time off, as mothers are today.

By then, conditions in the mill were starting to improve slightly and, in the eight years since I'd started, I'd already seen a few changes such as the breakfast break had been slashed and we now had a 10-minute break, morning and afternoon. We were given masks to cover our faces from the dust (although I preferred it without as I found it harder to breathe with one on), more modern machinery was coming in, which made the jobs easier and quicker (which, at the time, we didn't predict would end up going against the common worker) and we had a canteen, which was great because you got to know a lot of the workers from the different departments whose paths you might not otherwise have crossed.

So, all in all, it was great being back but

the distance to the mill put extra pressure on me getting home for Lynda and I also felt I was putting too much on Mum, expecting her to look after her grandchild all day.

'I don't mind,' she insisted, but I knew it was getting too much for her.

Mum was fine in the warmer months, but, even though she had retired and was no longer in the mill, her chest still played up the minute it turned colder. So, somehow, perhaps through my old friend Joan, I'd heard that Newroyd Mill, where she still worked, had a nursery, which I thought would be perfect for Lynda and it would take some pressure off Mum. It was also that bit closer to home, so better for me. Newroyd was a nice, smaller mill, run by a family firm rather than a corporation, and Joan still worked there, so she was the first I told when I found out they had work. In those days, it was quite easy to move from one mill to another. You didn't work notice like jobs today; you just finished up at the end of the week.

'That's great news,' said Joan, who like me was also a wife and mother now.

But it was sad breaking the news to my boss and fellow workers at Wye Mill that I was leaving.

'We'll miss you,' they said, giving me a hug.

I don't remember having a leaving do or anything like that, but I think they may have kindly had a whip-round for me.

'Ah, thanks,' I said. 'I'll miss you lot, too.'

But there was no time to mope, as come Monday morning I was at Newroyd Mill, 7.30am sharp. The mill seemed smaller than my previous one and darker inside; however, it was still three storeys high, with a huge entrance.

I knew I'd be doubling in here, which meant getting the fibres ready for spinning. But I didn't mind learning new jobs in the mill and, anyhow, it was still working in the card room, which I liked. It was harder work than I'd imagined, though, especially when I had to carry 17 bobbins on my arm!

'You'll be getting big muscles on those arms, lass,' joked the grinders. They were the male workers who tended to the back of the machines, which held laps of cotton far too heavy for a woman.

'I know,' I replied. 'I'll be stronger than you lot in no time!'

It was lovely being closer to home and, as we still lived with my mum, thoughts were now turning to getting a house of our own, but I had no idea where I'd get the deposit from. I'd seen a house I liked on Falkland Street.

'Ask the boss,' said Joan one day, while I

was sharing my woes. 'I've heard they help the workers.'

I'd heard the mill ran a holiday club, which meant you could take out so much of your wage and give it to them to save on your behalf, ready for your holidays.

But I never knew they'd do this too. So, one day, I bit the bullet and went in to see the boss.

'I've seen a house but I don't have the money so would I stand a chance of borrowing it?' I asked.

'Well, yes, right,' he replied.

They already knew if you were a good worker as it went through the books, so they could tell if you had a lot of time off and things like that. I was a good worker, or at least they must have regarded me as such. The boss agreed to lend me £300, for the down payment on the house, and we arranged a rate at which I could pay him back every Friday.

'If anyone asks, we'll just say you're paying into the holiday club,' he told me.

I suppose they were a bit like a bank, but it was my boss. You'd never be allowed to operate like that nowadays, yet, if it wasn't for him, I'm not sure when we'd have even been able to buy our house in Falkland Street. Mum would have been sad to see us go but she'd have never dreamt of holding me back. She came and visited as often as she could, so, although I missed her, we still saw a lot of each other.

As with the other two mills, I soon made friends and the banter was always flowing. And, although you'd be straight at your machine in the morning, and you didn't stop until the morning break, you'd always catch up in your lunch break.

I was enjoying it in the mill so imagine my surprise when I was told my weeks would be cut by one day.

'What's going on?' I asked Joan.

'I don't know, but I know I can't afford for my wage to drop,' she replied.

The bosses didn't say anything aside from the fact we had to do four days because there wasn't enough work. Of course, looking back, this was the start of the slippery slope towards closure, but at the time we didn't have any idea. I mean, we knew the mills had taken a knock because cotton was being made more cheaply abroad and now we had competition. After all, we'd seen the foreigners coming over and being trained and, of course, we'd heard about Gandhi's visit to Lancashire back in 1931 to see how it was done, but none of us ever imagined the industry finishing as it did.

So, once a week, I found myself at the Labour Exchange trying to look for more work, but I was hesitant about leaving the mill. Not only did I like the job and the people, but also the boss had been good to me. But when we were put down to three days, and then had a couple of weeks off and were told to go and collect dole money, because the manager of the factory had informed them of the situation, I knew I had to leave. At first I was happy to have the odd day to head home and clean but now it had gone too far.

'I can't survive on this,' I told Joan, so I went back to the Labour Exchange and found there was a card tenter job (a job I had done before) going at the Roy Mill in Royton, Oldham, so I took it. Mum was watching Lynda for me so that was fine until she was old enough to start school. This was a big mill but the windows seemed to have had a new lick of paint on them and the machinery inside looked a lot more modern. Not only did they have masks but they also had time-and-study people monitoring your output, too. We had a canteen, too, as most mills did by this time, and I used to love the cocoa, now better known as hot chocolate, especially as they gave it to us for free!

I was put in the card room, which I loved. In this mill they had the carder (boss of the department) and two under carders; Pat Porter was the one I reported to. I got on really well with Pat and his wife, who worked in the canteen. He was about eight years older than me, and whenever he had to work near to me we always got on well and had a laugh. Pat was a genuine, kind bloke, who was very comical and liked a joke.

I remember I hadn't been there that long when he came around, selling raffle tickets.

'Come on, for a worthy cause,' he said. 'You'll win a good prize.'

'What is it?' I asked, as others dug deep into their pockets for some spare change.

'It's a mystery parcel, which you take as it comes,' he smirked. So we all bought tickets and someone by me had won. A few days later, over came Pat, carrying this shoebox wrapped up.

'It's heavy, so be careful,' he warned, passing it over.

But when the bloke opened it, he looked inside to find bits of machinery! Pat and everyone fell about laughing, as we knew it was just a prank, yet the money would have gone to a worthy cause.

However, while there was still laughter and joking going on in the mill, an undercurrent of worry had also started up. We'd heard about the odd mill closing, but as the bosses never said anything we just hoped, and prayed, that the rumour mills were just that.

By then, I'd split with Jim as he'd turned into a bit of a drinker and I didn't want that for Lynda or me, so I was bringing her up by myself and the last thing I needed was to be out of work. One dinnertime, I was outside having a walk with my mate around the yard, as we often did when it was nice, when we spotted a row of cars parked up.

'That's queer,' said my mate. 'There's something going on here.'

I mean, it was only ever management who drove to work so at the most there'd have been a couple of cars but there was double the number that day, as if very important people had come to visit for a reason – and, sadly, neither of us felt it was a good one.

Although nothing was said at work, I went home with an anxious feeling and, when I turned on the TV and saw our mill on telly, I almost died.

'What the...?!' I gasped.

I can't remember now if it was the local news or a programme about the threat of closure of the mills but the manager from our mill was on, saying it was happening to us. I couldn't believe it. There were pictures of mills on the TV – I'd got a second-hand one a couple of years into my marriage – because we couldn't send out as much cotton as we should be (and had been), and there was someone from our mill explaining how it cost too much to export it. They were still buying cotton from abroad and then we'd manufacture it, but one of our managers was saying, why do we have so much of the stuff brought in here when we can't sell it abroad? It was clearly the start of the decline.

Well, the next day, the workers played hell and we waited for the manager to come into the card room. One by one, all the workers turned off their machines in protest. They'd never have done that before but everyone wanted answers.

'If it was going to be on TV why didn't you tell us?' they fumed. 'What about our jobs? How will we get another?'

Not surprisingly, panic spread throughout the mill when the thought of people losing their jobs became a reality.

'You can have time off to go look for work elsewhere,' the boss said.

Now, although we were grateful for that, the reality was the mills were closing so, even if we got another job, how long would it be for?

I'm afraid this is where it all gets a bit messy. I remember going from mill to mill as I chased work but I was never long in each mill and at one point I ended up working in an old people's home for a short while. During this time, I was in town when I bumped into my old boss, Pat. It was great to see him again, although I was deeply saddened to hear he'd lost his wife. As I told him about splitting with Jim, we chatted for ages and decided to meet up, just as friends.

Then, I'm not sure how, but around the same time work came up at the Roy Mill, as a lot of their workers had left after the threat of closure and found a job elsewhere. Pat was still there so it was great to have a laugh with him and soon our friendship turned into something more as we spent increasing amounts of time together. I'm not sure if other workers guessed but, if they did, nothing was ever said. After all, over the years, plenty of romances had started in the mills so we were hardly the first!

But, while Pat and me were falling in love and arranging our wedding, the mill was falling to pieces and the end was announced in 1978, not long before my 50th birthday. To this day, I'll not forget the sight of grown men crying. It was utterly heartbreaking. Whole families were affected by just this one closure, as it was common for families to all work in the same mill. I know there was one family where the father, mother and children all worked in that mill and another one had the grandmother, mother and daughter there.

'I can't believe it's come to this!' I sobbed. The thing is, we weren't just crying for our jobs but for the end of an era. For some workers, the mill was all they knew, and veering towards retirement age how could they possibly learn anything else for their last few years of employment? Plus, I knew some employers thought the men were too weak to employ in the later stages of their life.

As people left, this time there were no leaving drinks or bouquets of flowers presented for good service; they just went with a heavy heart. It was awful saying goodbye. Half the people I knew I'd not see again as it was uncertain where they would end up working – if they did at all. When the mill, and others that soon followed, closed, it wasn't just the job those people lost but also their purpose in life.

I carried on right to the very end. I think Pat had already left and found work helping out at a technical college, so there were about four or five of us left and we just ran through the last bits of cotton and finished it off. And then, silence, as we switched off the machines.

'Well, that's it then,' I said.

After leaving the mills, I got another job in an old people's home and then at Ferranti Technologies, an electronic manufacturing company in Oldham, where I worked until I was 59. I didn't mind it but from starting in the mill at 14 I always assumed, and hoped, I'd work there until my retirement.

Pat and me were married in 1978, just before my 50th birthday and not long after the Roy Mill closed. We moved to Hurst Green in 1994 to be closer to my daughter,

Lynda, but two years later Pat passed away from heart trouble. Sadly, Mum had already passed away so she never got to meet Pat, but I knew she'd have liked him.

Even though I was no longer working in the mill, I still kept an ear open to what was happening and I felt saddened as I heard each one I'd worked in had closed. It was to be expected, but it was still upsetting. I kept in touch with some of my friends via cards and letters but over the years the contact got less and less until it stopped altogether.

I'll always look fondly on the mills and I don't regret going in them, or wish I'd done something else. Not only did I make some great friends there but I also found my wonderful husband through them; they gave women a good job and the camaraderie of the workers carried everyone through, which was why it was so upsetting, seeing families out of work when the mills closed.

I wouldn't have wanted Lynda to go into the mill for the same reasons as my own mother didn't want me to, because of my health, but I'd tell her to try it to see how she went. My chest is bad now and I think I've got asthma. And I blame it all on the dust in the mill, but I don't feel hard done by; I loved my days in the mill, and, if anything, I just felt cheated that I didn't have more of them.

Grabbing my fent, which was a piece of cloth you wore to protect your clothes from getting snagged, I tied it around my waist and set my four looms to work. And the minute the clatter came, I was already counting down the hours to getting home.

Part Two:

Audrey Waddington

CHAPTER FIVE

Crushed Hopes

It was just light as I trotted down Jubilee Street towards Friendship Mill. It may have been close to 7am but it was still fairly quiet in the village. Like most mornings, I'd not said much to Mum and Dad, nor to my 13-year-old brother Geoffrey, and today in August 1945, it was no different. I wasn't a morning person – especially for the first half hour until I'd had my brew and come round. My 16-year-old sister Marjorie had already left for the mill because her weaving shed was outside the village and she started earlier; the two younger ones, Joyce and Ann, were probably still sleeping.

So, as usual, I'd woken up (automatically – we never had an alarm clock and I don't recall Mum ever waking me), splashed my face in cold water, pulled on my skirt and jumper, tied my auburn, shoulder-length hair into pigtails and left my face make-up free, before making myself some porridge (always with water and a pinch of salt).

I'd headed out onto our street, and walked down past the row of terraced houses. It was too early for the kids to be going to school and most of the mill workers were already at their looms, hard at it. I suppose there was an advantage to being only 15 – it meant I didn't have to start weaving at 6.30, unlike most in the shed! But it was only momentary relief as the minute I turned onto Whalley Road, the main road through the village, and glimpsed the tip of the slanted glass roof, my heart sank at the thought of another day in that place. I'd only been in the weaving shed for five months but already it felt like five years! Minutes later, the tall stone wall shielding the mill loomed closer and soon enough I was walking through the iron gate entrance and inside the single-storey shed to start another long day weaving.

Passing the engine room, I walked through the long passage to the shed, and, on clock-work, the clatter-clatter of the looms hit me. Heading down the alleyway to my own looms, I smiled at some workers en route.

'Morning,' I mouthed.

'Morning,' they mouthed back.

And that was that for the morning catch-up! There was no gossiping over a cuppa, unlike factory workers today. Not only could you not hear much, but also time was money in that place. And I hadn't really made any friends in there, to be honest, so it wasn't something I was inclined to do anyhow. I was there for one purpose only: to make money. And as far as I was concerned this job was a means to an end and that was all. The sooner something better came along, I was off!

Grabbing my fent, which was a piece of cloth you wore to protect your clothes from getting snagged, I tied it around my waist and set my four looms to work. And the minute the clatter came, I was already counting down the hours to getting home. But at 15 years old this was the reality of my life and, for now, I couldn't do anything about it.

At that time, my name was Audrey Davies (it's now Waddington). I'm 84 now, but even after almost 70 years I can still feel that sense of detest and dread at working in the mill. Looking back, however much I hated being a weaver, it provided me with a reliable income, though. And, over time, I used the mills to my advantage, dipping in and out of them whenever it suited me.

But just because I didn't enjoy my time in the mills doesn't mean I can't see their value, and it's an honour to share my story for, despite not liking the mills, they are still a part of my past and therefore important to me. The mills were an invaluable source of income for most people – especially the women in our village as it was mainly women who worked in the weaving sheds. I know some people loved working in there – my sisters did – but it just wasn't for me. And it wasn't the hard work or the conditions. Obviously, it was tiring, being on your feet all day, and I didn't cherish the non-stop noise of the looms or the general conditions, but the reason I didn't want to be in there was purely because I was bored out of my skull. I never had any preconceptions about myself but I was someone (and still am) who thought for herself, with a determined mind. For me, the mill gave me a trade, which meant I could be flexible when I worked and that was all.

Mum and Dad didn't work in the mill so it wasn't as if I'd heard any horror stories about the place. And most of the mums of my friends at school, and in some cases their dads, worked in the mill, too. But it wasn't just that. Despite being the biggest source of employment back then, working in the mill had never crossed my mind: I was never going down the mill, I always wanted better.

At the time of starting in the mill, I'd been living in the village for 13 years and the Second World War, although still happening, was due to end three months later. I didn't have any high expectations – women didn't then. You either went to college to study shorthand, worked in a shop or went into the mill. But for some reason I didn't want to do any of those things, especially not the mill. Despite living five minutes from a mill, being a weaver was never my idea. But when I was 14, what I *did* want to be finally came to me.

'I want to be a baker,' I told Mum and Dad.

'*What?*' said Dad.

'An apprentice baker,' I said.

It was April 1944 and I was due to leave school any day. Back then, when you reached 14, you could leave at the end of the summer, Christmas or Easter terms. So, with just a couple of weeks to go, my mind had turned to work. Like I said, I was well aware of the weaving shed in the village – in fact, we had two, the other being Victoria Mill at the other end of the village – and, with our Marjorie working at Longsworth Mill in the nearby larger village of Whalley, I was determined not to go in it. I loved baking and wanted to do that. I'd been helping Mum bake and cook since I was knee-high and that's what I wanted to do. In fact, I wanted to do cake decorations.

As usual, Mum didn't comment, as it wasn't like she had any say in it – Dad's word was law in our house.

'Well, you can try,' he said, 'but all girls should learn how to weave. That way you'll always have a job at your fingertips.'

It's funny now thinking back to that comment, because at the time Dad was right. And back then no one ever imagined or could predict how the future of the cotton mills would turn out. So, for then, he was right. All he wanted was for me (and my siblings) to have a trade, a job where (he thought) there would always be work. I respected him for that and completely understood why he was so insistent on it.

'So, if there aren't any apprenticeships in the bakehouse, you're going into weaving,' he added.

'OK,' I agreed.

I couldn't argue with him (not that I would!) for I knew he was right.

The next day, once I was home from school (St Leonard's in Padiham), I called into Brennan's, the village bakehouse at the bottom of our street. The bakery was located on Whalley Road, the main road through the village. It's still there today and aptly called the Village Bakery.

'Have you any apprenticeships?' I asked the man behind the counter. I wasn't sure if he was the owner or just someone who worked there.

'Afraid not,' he replied. 'Just taken someone on.'

'Oh, OK,' I sighed. 'Thank you.'

The chap took my details but, with a heavy heart, I walked up the street back home. I was determined to do anything but go in the mill, but what? So, the next day I went to the Labour Exchange, which was the place where you found work. Introduced in February 1910, it's now known as the Jobcentre Plus.

Being wartime, many women worked in the munitions factories, so, when the man in the Labour Exchange told me they needed people to make ammunition boxes at a wood-making place in Padiham, I jumped at the chance. Back then, you didn't have an interview; you just got given a piece of card with a name of the person to report to and went there. It was at a wood place called Winchester Works on Grove Lane, which was being used for munitions while the war was on, as it was May 1944.

Back home, I told my parents that I'd got work. The hours were 7am to 5pm but, because I wasn't 16, I didn't have to work Saturday mornings. I was to be paid £1 for the week, which I tipped to Father, and he gave me sixpence out of every half crown. After all, it was what we had to do as the family needed the money. Marjorie did the same and, once our Geoffrey was earning, he too would give Father his wage.

The next morning, I caught the bus for the short journey to Padiham. I just wore my normal clothes and tied my hair in pigtails as usual. The building was a few storeys high and I had my own workstation among mainly men and some women, all between their 20s and 40s.

I was so innocent then that, when the workers started with their colourful language, I couldn't stop blushing. The men soon cottoned on to how naïve I was and so they teased me with rude remarks. But it was all harmless fun and just the way it was in there. I was more shocked when I heard swearing – especially from the women! We may have been poor but there was never a swear word spoken in our house. Mum and Dad had nothing, but we were brought up to have good manners, with no swearing or drinking allowed in the house. Although I say swearing, it was nothing like the language today, just 'bloody' and 'blasted', but, for me, at that time, it was shocking enough.

But it was a delight working in there and I had such a laugh. Every dinnertime we had an hour off, and most days the guys would jump in the chute that travelled down through the building.

'Go on,' said one. 'It's just like a slide!'

'OK,' I said. I wasn't scared and I was a bit of a tomboy, so I thought this was great fun.

'I love it,' I told Geoffrey, back home. I always got on with my brother like a house on fire (Marjorie had her own friends so I never really bothered with her).

But the D-Day Landings in Normandy on 6 June 1944 triggered the beginning of the end for Hitler and raised hopes that the war would soon be over. So, eight months later, in February 1945, I was no longer needed. Although delighted the war was finally coming to an end, I was gutted to leave the place as I knew it meant only one thing.

Off to mill I go, I thought.

I kept nipping into the bakery but still they didn't have any apprenticeships so there was no other choice: I had to do it.

The next day I headed out towards the mill, but despite the chilly weather I didn't have a coat to wear. None of us ever had one and I just went outside in my jumper or cardigan without a second thought, as I didn't know any different. Once there, I found the office and spoke to a fella in there, who I assumed was the manager.

'Have you any jobs learning to weave?' I asked.

Now, like I said before, there were two mills in Read but I'm not sure why I went straight to Friendship Mill, but probably because it was at my end of the village. I don't know what I'd have done if they'd said no.

'Aye, we do,' he replied. 'Hours are 6.30am to 5pm, with an hour for dinner at 12. How old are you?'

'Fifteen,' I replied.

'Oh, well, in that case, you start at 7am – that's the law!' he said. 'But you can start as soon as possible.'

If memory serves me right, I think I

started the next day as I had to visit the local cobbler to get myself a pair of clogs. They were the customary footwear for weavers because you needed something comfy and good for your feet if you were standing all day – especially on the stone flags, which they had in Friendship Mill. In some mills they had duckboards so your feet were raised above the flags, not walking on them.

That morning, I doubt I jumped out of bed. I pulled on my knee-length skirt and jumper and tied my hair in pigtails (I didn't have a hairnet or anything like that and I don't recall anybody else in the mill wearing one).

At 7am sharp, I turned up at the manager's office.

'Follow me,' he said. He led me down this long passage before turning left into the weaving shed. I don't know if I was more surprised at how big the place was, the amount of looms in there or the noise! There was row upon row of identical looms, just inches apart, which seemed to stretch on for miles so I couldn't tell you how many were in there. The room was massive and in my eyes seemed bigger than our street! I didn't know where the workers could stand as there didn't seem to be enough room. The looms were powered by leather belts from overhead cross shafts on bevel gears from the line shaft running the length of the shed. The ceiling was slanted and split between glass and brick, to allow light for the weavers. I soon found out that weaving sheds were mainly single-storey with solid stone floors because the machinery was heavy and even noisier.

To me, most of the women looked old (in truth, they probably seemed older than they actually were, through my youthful eyes) and I didn't see anyone my own age. A couple of women looked up and smiled, but mainly they all had their heads down carrying on with their work. Then again, I didn't know anyone who worked there who was my age but I still expected to see some younger faces, I think. But one thing they all had in common was the big piece of cloth wrapped around their bodies. And they didn't have much room between the looms, just a few inches.

Now, because our Marjorie already worked in the mill, I knew a little bit about it. My sister and me weren't close to chit-chat, but she did tell me that you were put with a weaver when you first started.

'They train you,' she explained. 'It's usually someone who's been there ages because it has to be someone experienced and you must learn quickly because having a trainee with them means a loss of income as they are all on piece work [when you're paid by what you produce].'

I'm not sure how long it took Marjorie to

learn but it felt a lot of pressure having someone else teach me while they were trying to
earn a living too. So I was a little confused
when the manager walked me through the
hustle and bustle and we headed to the top
right-hand corner of the shed where four
looms stood empty, apart from one lady, and
the noise was far less severe.

'You'll learn here,' he instructed, leaving
me with the woman.

'Oh, right,' I said.

'Hello,' she smiled.

Now, at the time, this seemed quite a
pioneering thing to do, and, although I was
still unhappy about being in the place, being
trained in this way was far more appealing
than what I'd imagined.

'You'll stay and be trained here until
you're able to work your own looms,' she
explained.

Sadly, due to my ageing memory, I can't
remember the woman's name, but I do recall
she was probably in her 20s and she was
lovely. She had rosy cheeks and beautiful
teeth, with wavy, mousey hair and wore a
white overall (no one else in the mill wore an
overall – and it certainly wasn't something I
could afford) over a twin set (top and fitted
skirt). She spoke very well and, just seeing
how she looked, I knew she was too good for
weaving.

'I'm also the medical person,' she added.

'So, if you have an accident or feel unwell, tell me.'

I'm not sure if she was a trained nurse or just knew first aid but, thankfully, I never needed her help in that area and I never saw anyone else have an accident or become injured either.

I was never told why I was being taught in this way and, of course, I never asked, but as far as I was concerned it was a blessing. I hadn't wanted to come into the mill so at least this was a nicer start to it, especially when I realised it was just me being trained, and seeing the machine in front of me I was doubly pleased.

For those unfamiliar with the job, a weaver worked on a loom, which was a device to make cloth. The process is done by intersecting the warp (thread running lengthways across the loom) and the weft (thread going crossways on the loom). And as I stared at the loom before me with all its different parts (the main ones being the warp beam, heddles, shafts, shuttle, reed and take-up roll), I soon realised you had to have brains to be a weaver – especially if the cloth had a pattern.

'The front of the loom is where the warp comes in and is woven into the cloth,' the woman explained. 'The completed pieces are cut off the loom (from the take-up beam) and taken for inspection. Once you work by yourself, you'll be running at least four looms.'

As I stared at the machine, she kindly explained a few of the parts to me.

'The shuttle is what makes the banging noise as it passes from one end of the loom to the other,' she said. 'While the reed is a metallic comb, which is made of wires; the gaps between them are called dents and these can accommodate one or more warp ends. And the warp beam, also known as the weaver's beam, is at the back of the loom and this is where the warp sheet is wound on.'

About an hour into my training, I suddenly heard all the looms come to a halt.

'It's breakfast time,' said my trainer. 'They have an hour.'

I asked if I could have a quick toilet break.

'Of course,' she said.

The toilets were at the other end of the building. Now, like I keep saying, we were poor but, despite having nothing, Mum kept a clean house, so when I walked in and saw the state of the toilets I was appalled. Grotty, they didn't smell the best and overall were not very nice. I don't think I'd ever been to the loo so quick in my life! And when I came outside and saw people having a cigarette I shuddered at the thought. But I soon found out that was what everyone did.

We didn't have a brew break during the day, just breakfast and dinnertime breaks, so those who smoked nipped out there for a fag. I classed myself as a smoker but not a heavy one. Besides I could only afford to buy one packet of Woodbines and that would have to last me all week – and there were only five in a pack – so I certainly wouldn't be wasting one of my one-a-day smoking out there.

As with the munitions factory, I would have to give Father my wage and, when he gave me some back, he'd say, 'That's your spending money and you do what you like with that, but, should you choose to smoke it, then don't come here and ask for more money for the pictures!'

When dinnertime came round, I headed home (there was no canteen in the mill). My first morning hadn't been as bad as I'd thought it would be as I found it interesting listening to my trainer and of course learning. Also, it was nice being in the corner, where it was quieter, as we could talk.

As usual, there was fresh bread made (Mum made it every day) when I got in, so I made myself a brew and had the bread with some jam.

'Good morning?' asked Mum.

'OK,' I shrugged. 'I've got a lady teaching me to weave but, unlike our Marjorie, I'm not with a worker; she is nice.'

Mum and me never had big chats, but back then people didn't. I was enjoying the peace and quiet and she would have had more baking or food to prepare, as she always had tea ready on the table for when Dad, and now Marjorie and me as we were working too, walked in.

Back at work that afternoon, time went quicker than I imagined it would as the trainer taught me how to tie knots and put threads in, followed by how to find the right place when the weft breaks.

'If everything is running smoothly you just need to walk up and down, checking your looms,' she explained. 'But when you see that a shuttle is emptying, try to keep it so your cotton finishes at the end and, as quick as you can, take it off and replace it with a new one. That way, you'll then have a full length of thread, which will be flawless.'

'Thank you,' I replied.

'And just be careful of the shuttles,' she added. 'It doesn't happen very often but there's the danger that they can fly out – and you don't want to be clobbered by one!'

Oh great, I thought, *I've come to a death trap.* But I'm pleased to say I never accounted for an accident in this mill or any others, and I don't ever recall seeing an accident – especially not one caused by a flying shuttle.

By the end of the day I was ready to get

out into the fresh air (it was humid in the mill) and, even though we could speak, it was nice to escape the incessant clattering of the machines. The training woman had been lovely and I felt like I'd used my brain, but there and then I still knew that it wasn't the job for me and I wouldn't be staying there. As soon as I could leave, I would.

As the weeks went by, I was still being trained. It was nice being on a one-to-one with my trainer. And, as such, she was the only person I spoke to. None of my friends worked in the mill and every breakfast and dinnertime I went home, but I didn't mind. I hadn't gone to the mill for the camaraderie that some of the other workers had. I was there for one purpose: to get a trade. For me, it was just a means to an end.

She'd often leave me to it or ask me to weave her a pattern and then come over and check on me. One Monday morning, before we started, I noticed her covering her left wedding finger with tape.

'Oh, that's nice,' I gasped, cooing over the fine gold ring she was wearing – and about to cover.

'I'm engaged,' she smiled. 'And I don't want it ruined.'

It's funny, as, although we got on well, we never chatted any more about it or anything else besides work.

But the one piece of news that brought everyone in the mill together was hearing on the radio the Second World War in Europe was over on 8 May 1945. And, although there was no celebration as such in the mill, there was a feeling of overwhelming relief and pride. As the whole of Britain celebrated in the village, there were vast street parties and bonfires for Victory in Europe (VE) Day.

Not long after the celebrations had calmed down, my trainer told me, after three months of training, that I was ready to have my own looms.

'You're a fast learner,' she smiled, 'so I think you'll be fine with four looms.'

I know it had taken my sister Marjorie longer but she'd been taught by a woman trying to earn at the same time – I suppose I'd been lucky. The more looms you had, the more money you could earn.

Walking to my looms, I saw I had two in front and two behind, with just a few inches between, and I was shocked at how little room there was! Because you are sort of contained by your looms, I didn't really have much contact with the workers around me, but one of the older women close to me mee-mawed (mimed) for me to go get a fent.

'*What?*' I asked.

She pulled at the piece of cloth tied around her. When I nipped over to her, she shouted in my ear, 'It stops your clothes catching and plucking on the sand roller.' (The sand roller was at the bottom left of the loom and was like a grater, so, if you caught your skirt or jumper, it'd be ruined. That's why everyone in there was wearing one.)

'Where from?' I asked.

'Oh, just grab some wherever you can see some spare!' she smiled.

Everybody signed or mee-mawed in the mill so I knew it was something I'd have to learn. And as all the machinery set to work and the clatter grew noisier and noisier and I couldn't hear myself think, I knew I'd have to learn it fast! I wasn't very good at lip reading. For example, if you couldn't see the clock, you'd do a sign for clock/time and, to say you liked something, you'd stroke your cheek and point to the thing, such as someone's hair or the top they were wearing.

Now, despite all the machinery in the mill, it wasn't something I was afraid of. In fact, what I feared most was a fire. Soon enough, cotton dust started to fly everywhere. Bits of fluff would be in your hair and when the sun shone through you'd see it on your body. Today, they'd probably make you wear a mask but back then there was nothing of the sort and not such strict Health and Safety regulations. Soon, I couldn't believe how much dust had gathered under my looms so when the chap sweeping his broom came towards me I was relieved.

'Hello,' said the old man.

'Morning,' I replied, as he swept away the cotton.

The blasted stuff got everywhere, but what I was more worried about was it setting alight. You see, because we had iron on the bottom of our clogs, they could cause sparks owing to the fine dust from the cotton. It was like setting a match to it! So, each day, when one of the men came over to sweep the cotton fluff away from underneath, I was grateful, especially as they were so nice – unlike the tacklers!

In our mill, weaving was mainly a women's job, although the odd man did it too. But the men who worked in the mill were mainly tacklers – and I hated them! There were about four of them and they were maintenance men who came and fixed your loom. They weren't young because they had grey hair but to me they might have seemed older than they actually were. I soon took a dislike to the tacklers. They were horrible, very rude men. I don't mean in the way they swore – I never heard bad language in the mill – more that they were rude in an arrogant way. They were old school in their attitude, in that they thought it was beneath them to talk to me. I think it was a combination of me being a woman and younger, but that's just how it was and I suppose you could say they were snobs. It's odd thinking about it now because they wouldn't be allowed to act like that today; they'd be disciplined.

They used to wear a blue overall, a one-piece like a jumpsuit. They'd congregate in their little room inside the engine room, to the right of the mill as you first walked in. I used to dread anything happening with my looms.

Oh, no! I'd sigh, knowing I'd have to go and get one of them.

Walking towards the engine room, I peered round the door and saw them sitting there. The room was lovely and warm and they had a cosy little spot.

'I need some help,' I would say.

But they'd just look back at you: they wouldn't even acknowledge you, never mind react to what you'd said, so half the time I never knew if they'd even heard me. But all the tacklers knew where we worked, so, while I turned on my heels and strutted back to my loom, soon enough one of them appeared. Anyhow, I was frightened of them and we were always taught that we should never answer our elders back or call anybody by their first name so it was always Mr or Mrs – another reason why I didn't like it.

One more thing about the mill was I soon learned how tiring it was. You had to walk up and down checking your looms and the only sit down I got was when I went home for my dinner. I never had a brew break and trips to the toilet were rare as I was scared of leaving my looms and something going wrong, which meant losing money as you were only paid for the cloth you wove. You could ask people to watch them, and vice versa, but, although everybody's loom was technically the same, they were different in the sense that each one had its own quirks.

Saying that, I used to want things to go wrong (although I didn't like the bit when I had to get the tackler) because I soon grew bored of just walking up and down. That was my main bone of contention with the mill – it was so dull.

Once I knew what I was doing, I didn't find the work interesting. While everything was going as it should be, I found it boring as there was nothing to do aside from keep watching. Once the shuttle finished, you'd stop the loom and, as quick as you could, put another one in and get it going again. So I quite liked it when my thread broke or the thread had to be retied or pieced as it made my brain more active.

As time went on, I got to know a few more of the workers but I never had anyone I'd call a friend and, to this day, I couldn't tell you the names of those around me. Only people who came in from Padiham or the other surrounding villages tended to bring their lunch in with them, as most of the locals went home. And once you got the looms going that was it, no time for banter or chat.

Also, I didn't make friends that easily as I didn't have a lot of interest in other people unless they made an impression on me and I really took to them. I'd always been like that, and I still am today. So, I'd talk to a few of the women, at a distance, but no one ever became a good friend and I never had banter or a good laugh with any of them. Although Marjorie and me weren't that close, I knew she enjoyed Longsworth Mill and had lots of friends in there – I just didn't have that type of relationship with the people in my own mill.

I'm not sure if it was because they were older than me or I wasn't that bothered about making friends; they were lovely women and also pleasant to me so I wasn't upset by it – the opposite, in fact. I tried with the lip reading but I never really picked it up, so after a bit it was too tiring trying to shout over the constant banging of the shuttles and the clanking of the looms. All I kept thinking was that Dad was right: it might not have been my dream job but I did have a job at my fingertips and, for the moment, that's all that mattered.

CHAPTER SIX

A Tough Start

When I think back to how I grew up and had no other option but to go into the mill at 15 years old, youngsters had it so tough, unlike today. I was born on 4 April 1930 to Eva and Harold Davies. Mum was short with dark hair, while Dad was tallish and robust; I never saw him with hair. To this day I couldn't tell you how old my parents were when they had me, or the age they got married. That may seem odd now, but in those days it wasn't something you asked, and, sadly, I never did. Back then, it was just work, all work, and the man was the head of the house and his word was law. You didn't have idle chitchat around the kitchen table and talk. I'd never dared ask such a question: children were seen and not heard.

But what I did know was that Mum was an orphan and brought up in a home called St Deny's in Clitheroe before she left to work in service at a house on Henthorn Road in the same town. On the same road was the town's sewage works, where my grandfather (on my father's side, who was one of 13) was manager, so somehow their paths crossed and they got together.

When I came along, I was the third child born but sadly there were only two of us because our eldest sister Barbara had died at 18 months old. I was told (probably by Mother) that she had died from silent pneumonia but as an adult I questioned this and thought it may perhaps have been due to what we call cot death today.

Mum and Dad never talked about Barbara – it wasn't the done thing back then. So, for me, I only knew Marjorie as my older sister, who was 14 months senior.

I was born in a little cottage in Whalley, a village perched on the banks of the River Calder in the Ribble Valley. Dad was a driver and worked for Abbey Corn Mills, in Whalley, while Mum was a housewife. We lived in a one up, one down at Lodge Gates within the village Abbey. The one room downstairs was our living area and kitchen rolled into one and from there was a ladder that went straight up to the bedroom, where Marjorie and me shared a bed in the same room as our parents. There was a rail at the top to stop you falling, and Mum and Dad's bed faced the stairs, while ours was next to the window.

Although my memory of my first home is, not surprisingly, sketchy, it's actually my earliest, or first one – well, one part is. I remember getting tangled up in the bedclothes and screaming my tiny lungs out. Now, I don't know where Marjorie was or what time it was (it could have been day or night) but even at that tender age I remember feeling frightened and knowing I was stuck and needed help. Mum must have heard my screams as she finally got me out and I could breathe again.

When I was two, we left Whalley and moved less than three miles to the village of Read, to a two up, two down terraced on East Street. This house had a kitchen, living room and two bedrooms. I'm not sure why we moved as Dad still had the same job but I'm assuming it was because it was a bigger house. Now, somewhere along the line, we moved house again to Church Street, before finally settling in Jubilee Street. But, because this happened when I was a child, I'm afraid I can't pinpoint the exact dates, but my memory is mostly about Jubilee Street, where we lived second from the top.

Like our previous two homes in Read, this was also a two up, two down with a separate kitchen. Downstairs had the front room (best room, which we called the parlour), the middle room (living room) and then the kitchen. Both rooms had great big iron fireplaces with ovens so you could cook in either of them and the one in the front (which we thought was brilliant) had a tap to heat water on, as otherwise it was all done in pans in front of the fire. But furniture was bare and minimal. In fact, in the living room we only had a table and two chairs, and of course we had just the one bed for all us kids.

Being 1932, Britain was in a bad way as we were suffering from the effects of the Great Depression. Unemployment was high and had risen to around 2.5 million; poverty was widespread too. At that time, Britain had a class system of the poor, the intermediate and the upper class – and we were in the poor bit. Considering what was happening, I suppose we were lucky that Dad had a job, as things could have been a lot worse.

Read was home to two cotton mills located at either end of the village: Friendship Mill and Victoria Mill. Our house was about a five-minute walk from Friendship Mill. The mills were the biggest source of employment for the village (mainly for women as weaving was more of a women's job, although men did work there) and people from the nearby towns and villages, especially Padiham and Sabden, worked there too.

As I said, Mum was a housewife and Dad was a driver but because my parents didn't work at the mill I never really took much notice of it. And the social life of the villagers wasn't centred round mill life, as it may perhaps have been in other villages and towns, but the church. The mills were only there as a form of employment and nothing else, it seemed. Instead, Read was separated between the church and the chapel, and as a family we visited the chapel.

We never had new clothes: either they were second-hand or Mum made them herself. She had a sewing machine so, if she wasn't making stuff for us kids, then she was running up bits of clothes for the other villagers. But, despite not having much, Mum always made sure we were clean and tidy – especially on a Sunday to go to the Methodist chapel (to this day I don't know the name of it as we always said 'chapel'!).

Aside from the Sunday service, all social life revolved around the chapel. We used to have lots of social gatherings but I always remember Bonfire Night being the best. All the parents would go out and gather the wood, and those with old furniture they wanted to get rid of would throw that on the bonfire too – not that *we* ever had any! The mums would all bake mounds of meat and potato pies, while us kids shoved plot (now known as treacle) toffee into our mouths.

There was always harmless rivalry between church and chapel and, with Bonfire Night being a big deal, we never wanted any of the church lot sneaking to our bonfire once theirs had fizzled out. In fact, I remember we used to have lookouts at the bottom of the street to check and, if any of them tried to enter, they'd be stopped.

When I turned four, I attended Chapel School, which was two minutes from our house, and around the same time my brother Geoffrey came along (I don't have any recollection of Mum being pregnant or feeling anything about this). But once Geoffrey was too old to sleep in the cot, he was on a camp bed in the back bedroom with Marjorie and me in a bit Dad had partitioned off, with our parents in the front.

Now, because we had no bathroom (or running hot water), on a Friday each week we'd bathe in the tin bath, which was kept outside. We heated the water on the fire and bath-time was according to age, so I always went in after Marjorie. As I got older and my other two sisters came along, I always remember feeling relieved I was closer to the eldest as I wouldn't have wanted to get in at the end!

I hated having to share the water – especially with the thought someone may have peed in it – and it was something that stuck with me right up to becoming a mother myself. And, once we had a bathroom, I never ever shared bath water with my husband and sons. To this day, I refuse to do so. I won't share my towel with anyone or buy second-hand clothes either due to the fact that's all I wore growing up.

My sister Ann came along when I was five. Unlike the rest of our brood who all had auburn hair, she was blonde. As a bunch, we weren't a bad-looking family. And she too top-to-tailed it with Marjorie and me in the bed.

As I've said, Mum was in an orphanage, so the way she treated us was how I imagine she herself had been treated. We were well fed, and our clothes and ourselves were kept clean, but she never gave out cuddles.

One day, when I was about seven, Mum told Marjorie and me we had chores to do (Ann and Geoffrey were still too young, although I never saw Geoffrey do household chores, ever). I now believe she didn't know any better and that's what she herself would have had to do in the orphanage so she expected us to do the same.

'You must keep the front of the house clean,' said Mum. 'And you'll do it again if it's not right.'

I had to scrub each paving flag one by one on my hands and knees. And I'll tell you something, I did it without argument or question: in those days, kids did as they were told. So, once a week, when I came home from school, I'd do the chores. And, while I was on my knees outside, Marjorie had her sleeves rolled up while she cleaned the kitchen cupboards.

And, if scrubbing the path wasn't enough, I also had to keep the backyard and outside toilet clean too, and make sure my bed was made, as well as giving my bare-wood bedroom floor a scrub once a week, too.

After I'd done it, Mum would come out and inspect.

'Do it again,' she'd say. And I would, without question.

Now, I can imagine kids today would be horrified if they were told to do the same, thinking it was cruel or child labour – but it wasn't. Mum didn't know any different and I wasn't afraid of hard work. If anything, it made me a hard worker, something which has stayed with me throughout my life and I'm still the same today. I know that's why I keep such a clean and tidy house – and I clean my own paving flags to this very day!

I never knew if my friends at school had the same chores. You didn't ask things like that, and why would I? After all, it was my life and all I knew, so why question it? Besides I never had friends round to our house; it just wasn't the done thing, as we weren't encouraged to bring people round. And we had only two chairs so there wouldn't have been anywhere for them to sit!

Although we wouldn't have dreamt of not doing our chores, we still got to play out and have fun – only once they were done. Kids back then were innocent and we made our own entertainment. Often I'd play on the street with the other kids or Geoffrey and Marjorie. We'd play hopscotch, hide and seek and we'd even tie rope around one of the gas lamps and swing on it! Also, in those days, us kids used to go off walking around the village and roam the countryside without a second thought.

I often wondered what my mother did as Marjorie and me did all the work (Ann did chores too when she was old enough). Mum would bake and cook all day long, though. Every time I walked into the house, I could smell either the bread she had baked (she baked a fresh loaf every day) or the rabbit stew on the stove for tea.

I've already tried to explain how poor we were, but even so we were always well fed, so the last thing we suffered from was malnutrition (I was 11st when I was 12 years old)!

Now, I can't begin to tell you how much money Dad earned for driving but, considering we had nothing, it couldn't have been a lot. So I was extremely grateful that he kept a smallholding at the village allotments, about half a mile from our house. Dad rented out four pens but I haven't a clue how much he paid for them. But we had hens, goats, pigs, chickens and a vast greenhouse, where he grew tomatoes and veg. He also bred rabbits, which was a great asset as it helped to keep us.

'Needs skinning,' Dad would say to Mum as he walked in, holding a rabbit. I'd watch Mum skin, clean and prepare it fit for the pot. Being squeamish didn't even enter my head. It was just food that needed preparing. Seeing it turned into a tasty meal had me fascinated and I used to love watching her cook; the minute I was old enough, I'd help her. I believe that's what made me the good cook I am today, as I learned about food from a young age.

But, although our bellies may have been full, we didn't have anything else. Like I said, we only had the table and two chairs in the middle room (living room) and Mum and Dad sat on those. It's hard to believe in this day and age, but we had to stand on the hard flagstone floor (something I also scrubbed as part of my chores!) to eat our tea. And, even though we were standing, we'd still have to ask if we could leave the table once we'd finished eating. For the rest of the night, we'd remain standing as the whole family stayed in the room listening to the radio or playing games like tiddlywinks or snakes and ladders. Sometimes we sat down on the floor as I do remember a rug being there at some point. And it was funny as one day another chair just turned up out of the blue! It must have been a hand-me-down as I wouldn't have thought we had any money to buy one.

Despite our lack of wealth, Dad always gave us a Friday penny, which back then went a long way.

'Here you go,' he would say, handing one to each of us. 'Don't spend it all at once!'

Before he'd even finished his sentence, I was out of the house speeding down to the bottom of our street towards Brennan's.

Brennan's was a café and bakery but it also stocked sweets. And being the end terrace, it meant the window, which had the shelf with the sweets on it, faced out onto Jubilee Street – our street. So, each time I ran to the shop, I stopped outside the window and looked at all the sweets on show.

'Come *on!*' said Geoffrey.

Once inside, it took ages to choose.

'You do this every week,' sighed Geoffrey. 'Hurry up!'

I suppose we were quite spoilt as we didn't only get our Friday penny but we also got one from my neighbours on a Saturday, too. A nice, older couple, Uncle Bill and Mrs Hanson (I never knew why we didn't call her 'Auntie' and her first name), used to give me or my brother or sister a penny if we did errands for them, such as going to get their bread from the bakery. I don't think we decided who was going to go each week, I suppose it was whoever was first there.

'Wow, thank you!' I'd say, as Mrs Hanson

dropped a penny into my hand and I ran back towards the bakery to spend it all on sweets.

Mum and Dad ran a tight ship and by 8pm at the latest we'd be tucked up in bed under the flimsy blanket. Not wanting our fun to end, Marjorie, Geoffrey and me would play games in the dark.

'So, name every person on Church Street,' whispered Marjorie.

'Easy,' I'd snigger, rhyming off the names. 'Geoffrey, you do Fort Street.'

It's funny, thinking back, but because our village was only small we knew most people in it, especially those who lived close by and went to the chapel.

'Mr Hall, Mr Freeman...' continued Geoffrey, when suddenly we jumped out of our skins as we heard Mother shout, 'Come down here!'

'Oh, no,' I trembled, 'we're in trouble!'

As we scurried out of bed, we all knew what was in store. There, at the bottom of the stairs, Mum was holding the clothes brush.

'I *told* you to go to sleep!' she snapped. 'Hold your hands out.'

I put out my hands and she struck each palm with the wooden brush. And oh, how it killed! As I flinched with pain, I turned on my heels and dashed back to bed before she could see my eyes welling up. The last thing I ever did was cry in front of her, no matter how much it hurt. I don't think my siblings did either; we just took our punishment and got on with it. After all, it wasn't the first time we'd had it and it was certainly not going to be the last. And once the three of us were back in bed the last thing we did was talk!

Although compliant with orders at home, when it came to school, I suppose I was a little rebellious as I was always playing truant. There was a local farmer, an older man called Bob, who used to deliver milk to school in his horse and cart. Well, when he arrived, I would nip out of the class and go and jump beside him on the cart.

'Can I come for a ride?' I'd ask.

'Up to you,' he shrugged. 'But ya mum will kill ya!'

'I couldn't care less,' I said, trying hard to disguise the beaming smile that had spread across my face.

'Come on, giddy up!' Bob instructed, and as we trotted out of school I felt like a giddy kipper.

I don't recall Bob and me ever chatting. After all, what would we talk about, a young schoolgirl of about eight and an older man? Anyhow, I wasn't doing it to chat or make friends. Instead, I felt on cloud nine as the cart trotted around the country lanes of the village delivering milk to customers. Goodness knows who they thought I was! An hour later, we'd be back at the school.

'Thank you!' I cried, as I hopped off and ran back into school.

Bold as brass I strolled back into class amid the teacher's glare.

'Where have you been?' she asked.

Now, it wasn't that I didn't like my teacher and I wasn't trying to be bad or give her cheek, I was just craving a treat. And, sadly, the teacher – despite putting carbolic soap on our tongues if we said 'damn' – had no control over me, or the other pupils in her class, so she was never a deterrent.

'Out on the horse and cart,' I replied.

I think she must have told me that she'd been to see my mother (we only lived two minutes from school so it was quite possible). And the minute I walked through the door at the end of my school day, I knew she had as Mum grabbed the clothes brush and hit the back of my legs with it.

Again, though I winced with pain, I refused to shed tears as I ran upstairs. After all, that moment of pain had been worth the hour of pleasure! I didn't care as I loved every minute of it; it was my treat. It was my playtime and after that I went a few more times – and got punished – but always on my own. I didn't want to share it; I wanted to have some fun. To my mind, I wasn't harming anyone and it was worth the hiding I got. Looking back, I suppose it made me the strong-willed person I am today.

Around the same time as my milk-cart adventures, my sister Joyce came along. I don't really remember much about how she was born or her being a baby, just that all of a sudden she was there. But at the time the thing that sticks in my mind is nits – or, I should say, *me* having nits! Back then, we didn't have TV so we had to do something in the evening and looking for nits became a favourite pastime.

Out of five kids in the house (granted, Joyce was only a baby at this stage and Ann was three), I was the one who always had them, which was why my hair was always kept short.

Mum would never let me grow it and instead just stuck a bow in it. Marjorie, Geoffrey and me would come home from school and, one by one, Mum would check all our heads religiously. As she went through each one with a nit comb, it would come to me and she'd sigh and say, 'Not again!'

'I'll get the disinfectant,' said Dad.

'Oh, no,' I cried, 'it stinks!'

But Dad would come into the kitchen with this big gallon and pour some in a saucer. Mum would grab an old rag and dip it in before dabbing it onto my head.

'I can see them!' she said. 'Well, this will get them.'

As the other kids jumped away laughing, I could never understand why I was the one to always get them.

Soon enough, my thoughts turned away from head lice when, in September 1939, the Second World War broke out. I was just nine years old at the time. Now, although the threat of war was horrendous, at that age I found it exciting as I didn't know any different. As I've said, we always listened to the radio (a battery one charged by an accumulator), which back then would have been the BBC so we heard it all on there.

I can't ever remember Mum or Dad actually explaining what was happening so I didn't really understand, but I knew when a siren went off we all had to go under the stairs into the cellar.

'Quick!' shouted Mum. Grabbing the Tilly lamp (a portable oil or paraffin lamp), she hurried us all down there, where we perched on a big slab.

'How long do we stay in here for?' I asked, more concerned about the cockroaches scurrying about than a bomb being dropped.

'There's loads of them!' I screeched.

'Stop being a scaredy cat,' cried Marjorie.

'I'm *not!*' I shouted. 'Shut up!'

There was an air raid shelter in the village but we never went to it as we used the cellar instead. But the sound of the siren became a regular event. Sirens frequently went off as planes regularly came over towards the bigger towns and cities but, thankfully, it was never more than that. Our neighbouring village Simonstone was bombed but rumour had it that it wasn't a target but the pilot was simply off-loading on his way back, which was a common thing to happen.

There was no sense of fear but excitement whenever we heard a plane coming.

'Come on!' I'd cry to Geoffrey, as we darted outside and looked up to the sky.

'Who is it?' he called. 'Is it one of ours?'

For us, seeing the planes was so exciting as we'd never seen them before. But our planes had a different sound to the Germans: theirs was a noise like a revving sound, so, the closer it got and as we got a glimpse, Mum would call us back to safety.

'Get *in!*' she'd cry. 'It's the Germans!'

Even then, we'd rick our necks right to the last minute just to get a glimpse of the bomber.

As I've said before, Geoffrey and me got on like a house on fire. Marjorie had her own friend and, being a bit of a tomboy, I hit it off more with my brother. We went everywhere together. We'd hang out down at the Calder River, just having light-hearted fun. A favourite pastime then was collecting coal from the viaduct, which the Lancashire and Yorkshire

Railway line went over: as trains passed over on the slight bend, bits of coal would fall from the track. Goodness knows where, but we found an old trolley and would head there to see what coal was on the railway bank. Sometimes Marjorie came with us but usually just Geoffrey and me. It was such fun and like an adventure for us.

'Quick, put it in!' I'd order.

'Dad will be pleased,' he'd say, as it was ideal for the fire.

'Better wash your hands, though!' I'd giggle, as they were black.

We didn't have money, so any free coal we could get our hands on the better, and the more trains that passed through, the more we got.

And, if I wasn't having an adventure finding coal, the other pleasure I discovered at this time was smoking. And when I was about nine or ten I smoked for the first time. Well, I say 'smoke' in the loosest sense for my first 'cigarette' was actually just a rolled-up newspaper!

'Here, you try it,' said one of the local lads who hung out in our gang.

I don't think Geoffrey was with us as, in fairness, being two years my junior, he was a little too young for this. Anyhow, I reckon there must have been about three or four of us and one of them had rolled up a piece of paper real tight.

'Go on, try it,' he said, lighting it and handing it over.

Drawing it back, I began to cough my guts up.

'*Urgh!*' I spluttered. 'I hope the real ones are better.'

But that was just our practice run and it didn't put any of us off. And, after a few practices, we put money together to buy a proper cigarette – and it tasted so much better.

While most people struggled with rations in the war, we were lucky in that sense. We may have been poor but because of the smallholding we'd always been well fed – in fact, that's what kept us going. And even before the war nothing was ever wasted in our house.

From the smallholding, Dad would bring in the chickens he'd killed. But unlike today, when you buy a chicken all ready to cook, then it was Mum who'd pluck, clean and prepare it. And she would even eat the chicken's feet! Dad had ferrets so we ate a lot of rabbit (again, it was always Mum who skinned them) and she would eat the brains from them and the sheep, and make broth and dumplings so nothing was wasted. Dad would shoot ducks, which Mum had to first pluck and then singe (the finer feathers, which can be tricky to pluck); during the war, they were eaten a lot. In fact, you'd never see a brook with ducks swimming on it because they'd all been shot! That's why today I won't eat duck as I can still remember having to spit out the pellets from where they'd been shot. And we didn't get a fresh hen, always one that had dropped off the perch with old age.

I didn't really know many men who had to fight in the war and Dad didn't. I'm not sure if it was his age or his job that stopped him but I know we were all grateful, especially as he made sure we were well fed. But, because of the rationing, someone from the Ministry of Food came and took control of Dad's pens. He was only allowed to have the one pen, and most of the eggs and all the pigs bar one had to be given away.

'Here you go,' he said. 'Go to the village with your sister and get the orders.' Dad had made a barrow on four wheels so we could go around the village taking orders for vegetables. I must have been about 12 or 13 as me and Marjorie, probably on a weekend, went round the village taking orders before delivering them the next day. There was a sense of community in wartime and no one wanted to see anyone go without and it wasn't as if Dad minded, as he got his pens and stock back after the war.

Even though we had the smallholding, we still got ration coupons like everyone else but I knew there were certain things I never saw, like bacon, so I had my suspicions Mum was up to something. At the same time, she started to behave differently. Mum had never smoked, and like I've said before she and Dad were very strict, so I'd never worn make-up and I never really saw Mum with any on – until now.

One afternoon, she suddenly appeared wearing red lipstick and she was wearing a scent too.

'What's that?' I asked.

'Perfume,' she replied. 'California Poppy.'

To this day, I don't know where she bought it from or how expensive it was, but at the time Dad was so busy driving or working on the smallholding he probably hadn't noticed and I'm sure she only did it because she could get away with it. She started going out in Whalley, as she knew people there, so I think, with Dad working all hours, she finally found some freedom that she'd probably never enjoyed before.

I'm not sure if she ever drank. There was never any drink in the house, apart from a bottle of port and sherry at Christmas. And Dad never said anything – well, not in front of us children. Anyhow, I often wonder if she was selling the coupons so she could pay for her beauty products and go out!

While our soldiers fought for our freedom, I was just growing up and doing what kids do.

I'd started at St Leonard's secondary in Padiham. I didn't mind school or the lessons, but my favourite was the gym or doing anything competitive. But what I loved more than anything was helping Mum to cook. As I've said before, I'd help out with tea, but what I preferred doing was baking. Mum made all her own jams, bread and pies. She and Dad would take us on picnics and we'd pick fruit and then bake it when we got home.

And the more I baked, the more the time crept towards April 1944, when I was due to leave school, and suddenly I knew what I wanted to be: a baker. But my main concern was how I'd achieve this ambition since the most obvious route for me was to go in the mill, as the last thing I was scared of was hard work.

Trouble was, the mill wasn't where I wanted to be.

CHAPTER SEVEN

Fulfilling My Dreams

Anyway, back to the mills. And with each day it didn't get any easier dragging myself out of bed for work. I think I just came to in the mornings, although sharing a bed with Marjorie, Ann and Joyce probably didn't help! Marjorie was always up sooner than me as she started half an hour earlier and had to get the bus to work.

After my usual morning ritual of splashing my face with cold water, getting dressed and making myself porridge (or even toast sometimes), I was out the door and doing the five-minute walk to the mill. Like I said earlier, I still hated the mill. Even though it was now August 1945 and I'd been there six months, I didn't like it any better – I just went in, did my work and came home. None of the friends I played out with worked in there.

So, the highlight of my day was dinnertime when I raced home to the aroma of Mum's freshly baked bread. But as I dragged my heels back to the mill – passing the bakehouse on my way – it just made me feel even more gutted that I wasn't doing what I wanted to do. It was always a joy to get out of that place after a hard day's work. Once home, Mum would have a rabbit stew or potato pie on the table ready for the workers – Dad, Marjorie and me.

Once I'd asked permission to leave the table, if I didn't have chores to do, then I would head out to play for a couple of hours before bed. In fact, it's funny now, thinking back, that at 15, when I was earning, I was still playing hide and seek around our street or hanging out in the woods. Compared to teens today, it was all very innocent, though.

There was a gang of us from the village and sometimes Geoffrey came too. But it was such a long time ago, sadly, I can't remember the names of the friends we played with, although we never did anything mischievous other than play games!

As previously admitted, I was a bit of a tomboy growing up. Dad was always tinkering with motorbikes and so one time I asked him if I could have a go.

'OK,' he said.

In fairness, I was fooling around a little and I don't think I really expected him to say yes.

'Really?' I asked.

'Well, get on then and I'll rev it up,' he told me.

It was a Norton 500cc and, as I sat back on the leather seat and gripped the handlebars, I giggled with excitement. He pushed me along to an unmade road, a mud track, not far from our home.

'Right, listen to what I tell you,' he said, as he fired instructions of what to do. And, before I knew it, the bike had shot forward and I was driving it!

'Careful!' he shouted after me.

I jolted a few times before I rode smoothly: 'I've got it!' I shrieked. I couldn't believe how easily I'd picked it up.

'Can I go again?' I asked Dad as I came to a sudden halt.

'Another time,' he smirked. 'I think that's enough for one day.'

After that, Dad took me out a few more times. It was only ever me that asked and it was nice to have time on my own with him as we had a bit of a laugh. I never went on the main road, as I never applied for a licence; I just went on the back lanes and I loved it! It was different in those days as there was no traffic, unlike today, so things like that could be done.

Now, because the bakehouse was on my way to work, I passed it a lot of times. But also, I'd go in to buy sweets or run errands for our neighbours, Mrs Hanson and Uncle Bill. Anyhow, I'd heard that someone in there was leaving, so I thought it was worth my while popping back in to check.

So, this day after work, I went in and saw that a smaller, younger man was serving behind the counter.

'Do you have any apprenticeships?' I asked him.

'We do actually, as someone has just left,' he replied.

I felt like jumping for joy! After introducing himself as Mr Sumner, he explained that he had taken over the business. He was from Fleetwood way and was married with a daughter; later he had a son, too. I'd have guessed he was in about his 30s; he was very nice.

'So, when can you start?' he asked.

'I can finish up at mill on Friday,' I told him.

I don't think I'd ever run home so fast! As usual, Mum was putting tea out on the table and Dad was sitting ready.

'Dad, you told me if I learned to weave then I could have the job of my choice,' I tentatively began.

'Aye,' he replied.

'I've done as you said, but now a job has come up in bakehouse so I'm leaving mill to work there.'

'That's fine,' he told me.

Now, back then, I don't think anyone would have congratulated me for getting the job I wanted. They were just pleased I was working and bringing money in – whatever it was from.

I couldn't wait for morning to come, and for the first time in six months I leapt out of bed for my day at the mill. Once there, I went in to see the manager.

'I want to finish end of week,' I told him. I tried not to sound so pleased, knowing I had only three days left in the place (in those days, there was no notice, you just worked until the end of the week and then left).

I forget the manager's name but he was only a short man, about 5ft. He looked old to me but I bet he wasn't. He was approachable, though, and I didn't mind him but, although he was nice enough, I don't think he wished me well. Anyhow, they'd spent all that time training me up and I'd left short of seven months later.

I probably told the few workers around me but that was all.

'Oh, good luck to you,' said the older man next to me.

'Thank you,' I said.

And of course there was no such thing as a leaving do as there is today; nobody had any spare cash for a collection. Besides I didn't expect one, given the short length of time I'd been there and the fact I didn't have that many friends.

I'd never wished my weekend away before

but, as far as I was concerned, Monday morning couldn't come round quick enough! I had to be at the bakehouse for 6am – even earlier than the shed – but I didn't care because I was going to a job I wanted to do. I don't remember Mum or Dad waking me (and of course we didn't have an alarm) but I got up no problem and it was such a relief, knowing where I was going to work.

I wore my usual uniform of a skirt and jumper, tied my hair in pigtails and slipped on my oldest pair of shoes, as I headed down towards the bakehouse.

'Morning,' Mr Sumner smiled. 'I'll show you around before you get started.'

The bakehouse was at the end of a row of houses so it had the shop front and then the middle room was divided between the living area for Mr Sumner's family and the prep for the bakery. In the middle stood a great big wooden table and a large machine for mixing dough. The kitchen was built out slightly to accommodate the industrial ovens needed.

Mr Sumner wore a white overall and handed me one, too. He was going to train me, but part of the job was also cleaning up.

'The table needs scrubbing every night,' he told me. But I didn't care: I wasn't afraid of hard work and I didn't mind cleaning. For me anything that wasn't the mill was a bonus!

As each day went on, I loved working with Mr Sumner more and more. Not only was he a great teacher, but he was also kind. And with each day I counted my blessings that I was there. Obviously, the mill was still in my life. I could see the roof on my walk to work, some of the workers came into the bakery shop and, of course, our Marjorie still weaved. But back then you didn't talk (or moan) about work, especially not around the table, so I never really talked to our Marjorie much about it. Unlike me, she seemed to like it in the mill and was even stepping out with some lad who worked there.

Things were so different back then. Even though I was on cloud nine, working at the bakehouse, I don't ever recall my parents or Marjorie even asking if I was enjoying it – you just didn't. But I wasn't bothered as I was just thrilled to be baking. And, while Mr Sumner showed me the basics, I was happy to learn, but all I really wanted to do was decorate the cakes; I loved how pretty the icing looked on little buns and birthday cakes.

'Don't worry, we'll come to that,' Mr Sumner smiled. 'You're doing well as you are. And don't bother with night school, I can teach you everything you need to know.'

He was so good to me, and so was his wife. In fact, the whole atmosphere was so much better. While Mr Sumner and me worked out the back, his wife and a shop girl called Iris (about my age) served in the front. Iris was a nice girl. Tiny, with curly dark hair, she wore dark-rimmed metal glasses and was from Padiham. Although we never saw each other outside work, she was also lovely to me.

Every day we'd stop for elevenses and Mr Sumner would offer me a plain teacake served hot with butter and sliced raw onion. I was in heaven!

'Oh, thank you,' I said.

Not that I was hungry as we could eat whatever we wanted, so I never bothered going home for lunch.

One day, Mr Sumner gathered Iris and me together to tell us some exciting news.

'Right, we are now going to have the canteen for Friendship and Victoria,' he announced.

Now, we both knew this was a big deal for him – and of course the business – as it meant a lot more custom. You see, neither mill had a canteen so Mr Sumner had applied for the chance to be the canteen, if you will, for both Friendship and Victoria so the workers had somewhere to come and get their dinner instead of going home or taking in sandwiches. That way, they could have their lunch in the café or just buy a pie or sandwich and take it back to the mill. And, although the war was over, certain foods were still rationed but this way his points (shops had a points system during the war) were more, so they doubled the amount of sugar, meat, etc., he got.

'So, because the café's going to be busier at lunchtime, would you like to waitress for me?' he asked me. 'And I will pay you for that separately.'

Mr Sumner knew I was tipping up to my dad so this way Dad wouldn't know I was working extra – and, more importantly, earning more. I could stash this extra wage and he'd be none the wiser.

'Of course I would,' I said, almost snapping his hand off. Like I've said before, I wasn't afraid of hard work – especially when it made me money!

Soon enough, come lunchtime I swapped my overall for a pinny as I waited on in the café. I never wore make-up, my parents were very strict and wouldn't allow it, and I kept my hair in pigtails as they'd been for baking. I was paid £2, and, as promised, Mr Sumner paid me in two separate wages.

Come Friday, as I handed Dad my wage, I still had the 10 shillings extra and, once upstairs, I hid it safely under my pile of clothes.

Mr Sumner's bakery and the new café were doing great. Every dinnertime, the café was rammed. At this time, a new set of council houses was being built on Read football field at the top of my street, Jubilee. So, as well as mill workers being in the shop and café, now a lot of builders and labourers who were working on Greenacres, the new houses, were coming in. But I never really took much notice of anybody; I just got on with my job, as, once my hour waitressing was finished, I was back in the bakehouse.

Because I worked Saturdays in the café and bakery, Mr Sumner always gave me Mondays off. One Tuesday, in July 1946, when I arrived, he asked if I knew one of the builders who came in.

'He always gets me to fill his flask with hot water,' he said. 'He is the boss but he always comes in for his dinner with a younger lad.'

'Err, I think so,' I said. 'Why?'

'Well, the young lad wants to go out with you,' he told me.

Well, I can't have been taking that much notice of what he was saying as I thought Mr Sumner was saying this young man wanted to go out with Iris, so I replied, 'Good for her! What's his name?'

'Jack Waddington,' Mr Sumner said.

'Well, she's not changing it much then, what with her being Iris Warburton!' I giggled.

'What you on about?' asked Mr Sumner, clearly confused.

'This lad wants to have a word,' I said.

'No, it's not Iris, it's *you!*' he replied, laughing.

'Oh, well, he can get lost!' I sighed. I'd not had a boyfriend before and I just wasn't fussed. Also, I wouldn't have dreamed of just going out with somebody I'd never met before; I had to get to know him first.

That dinnertime, I heard the boss builder shout my name. As well as the shop front, we had a hatch where people could place orders, and he was shouting through that.

'Audrey,' he yelled. 'Jack wants a word with you!'

'I'm not interested,' I told him, walking away. I don't know why I didn't even want to entertain the idea, but somehow I didn't.

Mr Sumner never mentioned it again, but a week or two later he was having some new furniture for the café delivered so he asked if I could help him carry it upstairs.

'I'll do what I can,' I said.

It must have been after dinner as there was no one in the café upstairs as I carried a chair up there.

With that, I saw the builder boss and Jack walk in.

'Would you like some help?' asked the boss man.

'Oh, I wouldn't mind,' replied Mr Sumner.

As I picked up another chair, Jack did the same and followed me upstairs. No sooner had we walked into the room and put down

the chairs than someone shut the door behind us. As Jack went to open it, he looked
embarrassed.

'It's locked,' he told me.

'*What?*' I said, trying the door handle.
'What's happened?'

'I think there's been a trick played on us,'
he smiled.

Mr Sumner and the boss man had locked
us in together so I'd talk to him. I couldn't
believe it!

'All I wanted to do was ask you if you'd
come to the pictures with me,' said Jack.

Somehow, I knew he was as mad as me
and clearly he'd had no part in the trick so
it wasn't his fault. And I could also tell he
was a nice person.

'I suppose so then,' I smiled.

Jack was 21 and lived in Burnley. He'd
been wounded in the war when he was 18. I
could never say he was handsome because
he'd been badly wounded and his face was
scarred. He told me it happened when he
was in Caen, France, during the D-Day
landings, and he and his troops were going
through a minefield; his friend had stepped
on a mine and lost both his legs. The blast
alerted the Germans and they began to
shoot out randomly so Jack got the impact
from the blast, as well as being shot in his
arm, face and legs. To the day he died, he
had a piece of shrapnel moving around his

body the doctors could never take out.

I knew Jack was conscious of his face but, to me, it was irrelevant. I was more concerned about what was inside, not his looks. Anyhow, I knew he was a perfect gentleman.

Soon, the door was unlocked and Mr Sumner and the boss man just looked sheepish. I don't think I said anything as Jack had turned out to be nice and I'd agreed to go to the pictures with him so I wasn't bothered.

A few days later, I met Jack in Burnley to go to the pictures. I told my parents I was going to meet a boy but they didn't say anything. I caught the bus from Read but I knew I must be home by 9.30pm at the latest (my parents were strict and there was no staying out late allowed). Now, back then, there was a picture house on every street corner, so I couldn't tell you which one we went to or what we saw.

Although going to the pictures was a popular thing in those days, it was still seen as a treat (well, to me anyway) as I knew I could never afford it. That first night, I think Jack paid, but again I couldn't tell you how much it was. And it was hardly the ladylike thing to ask a gentleman how much it was if he'd treated you.

It's funny because, although I remember being nervous, the conversation was flowing fine – we seemed to talk about anything and everything. I liked everything about him; he was such a caring, nice man. He told me he lived with his mum Maggie and his brother Harry. Sadly, his dad had died when Jack was only 11.

From that night on, we started courting and I saw him regularly. It's weird as, back then, once you had a boyfriend, you didn't really bother with your friends. Not that I had a lot of friends to begin with, but from then on all my spare time was spent seeing Jack.

'You've got a good one there,' Mr Sumner smiled.

'I know,' I said.

Jack used to cycle over to my house on his push-bike and other times I'd catch the bus and go to see him at his house. I got on well with his mum and brother. They were both weavers, but we never really talked about the job – I got the impression they didn't seem to mind it, unlike me, and had been doing it all their working lives. I also met Jack's sisters, Irene and Emma, who were both married, and they were lovely. I used to love going to Jack's and spending time with his family, as I got on so well with them all.

But, while I was slowing falling in love, sadly, Dad wasn't so enthusiastic about me courting a builder.

'He'll always be out of work,' he warned me.

Thankfully, Dad turned out to be wrong and, in all the time I knew Jack, he never lost a day's work.

Now, I never knew anything about the birds and the bees. In fact, I didn't even know where a baby came from. I knew it was from 'down there' but I didn't know anything else! So, the more me and Jack saw of each other, the closer we got – in more ways than one. And after a few long walks in the lovely summer weather I soon found out how you got a baby.

So, two years into dating, when I found out I was pregnant we decided to get married. In those days, being pregnant out of wedlock was frowned upon. Anyhow, we both knew we'd be married one day.

At the same time, Marjorie had got engaged to her fella, Ken. He was from Whalley and, as I've said before, they met in the mill. It was odd how we'd had such different experiences of the mill. She loved it – and had found love – unlike me, who had hated it.

Marjorie was getting married in July.

'Let's have a double wedding,' she suggested.

'OK,' I said.

Jack and me couldn't care less if we went to a Registry Office. We just wanted to get married now, but we knew it would go against the grain if we did that.

'So, we need to get you a dress,' my sister added. 'And quick!'

Marjorie's dress was made by our aunt Phyllis, a tailoress who taught at Blackburn College, but I just borrowed one from my friend Agnes.

Although I was excited about getting married, it meant I'd have to leave the bakery.

'I'm moving to Burnley,' I told Mr Sumner.

'I'm pleased for you,' he replied. 'And my present to you both will be a wedding cake.'

I was sad to go, but I knew we'd stay friends – and we always did.

The night before my big day, I just had my Friday tin bath as usual and went to bed. There was no such thing as a hen night in those days. And, on 17 July 1948, Dad walked me down the aisle of St John's Church, in Read, while our uncle Stan walked Marjorie down. I was three months pregnant but you couldn't tell.

We had the reception at the bakery café, which was lovely but nothing fancy by today's standard. And it helped having the same guests there for us both.

From the reception, we got changed and then caught the train to Blackpool for our honeymoon. We stayed in a lovely B&B and the first night we giggled nervously as we got into bed together and snuggled under the covers.

Just then, the covers were pulled off us, downwards.

'Jack, what are you doing?' I asked.

'Nothing,' he said.

But, each time we pulled the covers up, they were somehow dragged back down again.

'You must be,' I insisted. 'Our bedclothes are moving!'

'I'm not!' he said.

All of a sudden, they came right off and we heard giggling on the landing outside our door. Jumping out of bed, we saw the bedclothes tied to a rope, which went under the door – where someone was obviously pulling them!

Dragging on some clothes, we opened the door to find the couple who owned the B&B on their knees, laughing at their own prank, which they readily admitted they played on all the honeymooners.

Thankfully, we saw the funny side, too.

A week later, it was time to head home – but now home was Burnley, as we had moved in with Jack's mum.

'I'm married,' I smiled to Jack. 'That means I can do what I want, and Mum and Dad can't say anything.'

And the first thing I did before going to see

them was paint my nails and put on some lipstick – something I was never allowed to do!

'Hello,' I said, walking in. 'I'm back.'

They said nothing but I could see it all just by their looks. And for the first time in my life I was my own person and there was nothing they could say or do.

CHAPTER EIGHT

Back to the Mill

I quickly settled into life living with Jack, his mother Maggie and brother Harry at their terraced home in Harle Syke, a small village within the parish of Briercliffe, three miles north of Burnley (a prominent mill town and at its peak one of the world's largest producers of cotton).

I got on so well with Jack's – well, now my – family too. His mum was small, a little wide, and her dresses and skirts came right down to her ankles. She had iron-grey hair so I used to call her grandma because, although she was only in her 50s, she looked like one to me. I think it's fair to say she had a fiery temper but was a good woman. I thought she was brilliant and we got on very well, while Jack thought the world of her. His brother Harry was a wonderful man. A true gentleman (I never once heard him swear in front of me), he had blond hair and was a great personality.

Jack's family home was at the back of a butcher's shop. The butcher had the front room and the cellar, while our house was the back room, and upstairs. Although it was a dream come true to have a bathroom, because there were only two rooms, Jack and me took his mum's room (the biggest), Maggie moved into Harry's room and he moved into the bathroom! Thankfully, it was a big enough room to fit in a bed – and obviously we made sure not to have a bath when Harry was in!

Downstairs was a squeeze for four adults in the one room but we managed. We only had a sideboard, a table and three chairs. The wooden floor had a large square of coconut matting and beside the sink was a dolly tub (a metal ribbed tub filled with water) and posser (a three-legged pole with a handle to turn the laundry in the dolly tub) ready for washday.

Now, because I wasn't working I was happy to take over the housework. So, I spent my days cleaning and once a week doing the big washing task, which would take all day. But what I didn't mind was doing the cooking.

'That's delicious!' said Harry, as he wolfed down a meat stew. When he, Maggie and Jack had arrived home from work, tea was ready on the table.

'Thanks,' they said.

'It's nothing,' I replied. 'You've been hard at it all day, it's the least I can do.'

Harry and Maggie were weavers and worked in one of the many mills in Burnley.

My memory is not for giving me the names, I'm afraid! After Maggie lost her husband, she had no choice but to return to work full-time to bring in a wage. But that meant she wasn't at home to cook a hearty meal for her sons, apart from Sunday, when she made a roast dinner. Well, being at home all day, it was a pleasure for me to cook – especially given how appreciated it was.

It was all well and good, me cooking, but I needed a wage coming in. I'd had to leave the bakery because I now lived in Burnley and it was too far and too much of an early start to get there. And Jack was only earning £3-odd a week. That wasn't enough if we wanted our own house once the baby was born.

'Why don't you come and weave?' suggested Emma, Jack's sister. In her 40s, she worked at Queen's Mill in Burnley with her husband Ernie and had been there (or at least, weaving) all her working life (she didn't have children). Much as it pained me, I knew she was right.

Suddenly, Dad's words popped into my head: 'You'll always have a job at your finger-tips.' And he was right. I knew I could use the mill for some quick money, but I'd no inten-tion of staying; I could bring in a wage for at least six months so it was well worth it. In those days, the pregnancy allowance was six weeks before the birth and seven after (or you could choose to do it the other way round).

And at least this time I'd have family around me.

'Yeah, it's a good idea,' I replied.

'OK, I'll ask for you,' she said.

Back then, you didn't have an interview, and because I already had the experience, I wasn't at all surprised a few days later when Emma said I could start.

'Great,' I said, not meaning it.

I soon found myself walking towards the mill to start a day's weaving as it was only a short walk from home. And, as the 120-foot smoking chimney came into view, I realised my hatred for the mills hadn't subsided as I shuddered at the thought.

I can't believe I'm doing this again, I thought, still hating it, and I hadn't even got started yet.

The steam-powered mill was built in 1894, on high ground to the south of the River Calder in Harle Syke, a suburb of Burnley, with a single-storey building. It was originally of four-storey construction with a large weaving shed but, after a fire in 1918, it was remodelled into a single-storey building.

I think Emma must have met me and taken me in to see the manager.

'She can come with me for the day, until she gets the hang of it,' she offered.

'OK,' he said. 'Then you can take six looms. Hours are 7.30am to 5pm, and you'll

161

get £1 and 10 shillings a week.'

That was considered a good wage and would be about £1.50 in today's money.

Well, at least the half-hour later starting time was something! I didn't tell him I was pregnant, or that I would only be there for a few months. As far as I was concerned, it was nothing to do with him as I was only there to work while I could and I didn't feel at all guilty because I knew what I was doing, so it wasn't like they'd spend time training me. Anyhow, I don't think they'd have been bothered as they were happy to get a yarn of cloth for them.

Following Emma into the shed, it was no different to the last one with the endless rows of looms and the conditions seemed the same as Friendship Mill. From what I could see, nothing had changed – apart from the fact we started at 7.30am.

'This is nice,' she said, as she set her loom to work.

'Hello,' Ernie, her husband, smiled. 'You with us today?'

Forcing a smile, I didn't have the heart to reveal how I really felt. I'd never let on about my utter dislike for the mill as they both worked there and I'd never heard them moan about it; I thought it would be a disrespectful thing to do.

'Looks like it,' I smiled, grabbing some material to use for my fent.

Soon, the clatter of the looms started.

'I haven't missed this,' I told Emma (well, I mee-mawed it!).

Unlike the rest of mill, I still hadn't picked up lip reading. In fairness, I never put much effort into learning, as I think subconsciously I knew that I never intended to stay. Instead, I just mee-mawed and did the signs.

Most dinnertimes I went home, or the odd day I did bring sandwiches but, apart from Emma and Ernie, I didn't really make friends with anyone. Not that anyone had time to chat. I was there to make money so I made sure my looms were running, but I wasn't there to make friends or socialise.

Six months later, at the end of November 1948, I knew it was time to leave so I went in to see the manager.

'I'm leaving today,' I told him. I didn't have to give notice, and, although people did have collections, I didn't get one nor did I expect one. He didn't say much but I know he wouldn't have been pleased to lose a qualified weaver.

I couldn't wait to get out of there. But it was funny because, 25 years ago, I went back to the mill. Since its closure in 1982, it has been preserved as a museum. This time I actually enjoyed being there and thought it was fascinating to see the mill, especially the engine room. It's just a shame I didn't have the same sense of enthusiasm when I worked there.

That Christmas after I'd packed in at the mill, it was a bit tough as, with only one wage, we didn't have any money so we bought two rabbits from the butcher and made do with them. And I was ready for this little one to make an appearance so I could get back earning. I didn't want to go back to the mill once the baby was born but I wasn't sure what else I could do.

Putting it to the back of my mind, I tried instead to focus on the baby and, after a week-long labour, our son John was born on Saturday, 29 January 1949 at Bank Hall Maternity Hospital. Back then, you didn't have the dad (or anyone else) in with you and the midwives (who always called you 'Mrs'); there was only gas and air and a towel tied to my bed-end to pull on.

I loved my son and being a mother but after a while I got lonely being at home all day with a baby, as Jack and the others would leave home at 7am and not be back until 5pm – plus, I was only 18.

Now, I know the option to return to the mill was there but I was putting it off, when one night Jack told me they were looking for people to work the evening shift at Lucas Engineering, in Burnley, as a quality control inspector.

'I don't mind watching John, if you want to do it,' said Jack.

So I did, and I loved it.

'It's the best job I've had since the bakehouse,' I told Jack.

I liked having to use my brain and I loved the people I worked with, but we all knew it wasn't practical to have four adults and one baby living in such a small house so we had to think of something else. There were new council houses coming up for rent in Read, called Greenacres. In fact, it was the site where Jack had been working when he used to come into the bakehouse and asked me out. I knew it would be nice for John, us being back in the village, and if we had any more kids too. By then, Mum and Dad had split up and Dad had moved away, so it meant there was space at home as Geoffrey was now in the RAF and there was only Mum, Ann and Joyce left there.

'We'll make room,' said Mum.

So, in January 1953, I was heartbroken to say goodbye to everyone at Lucas's and to leave Maggie and move back to Read.

'I'm going to miss that place so much,' I told Jack.

It was nice being back in Read and living with my family again. And Mum let us three have the front room. No one knew where Dad had gone so I didn't pry. But good news followed our move when I found out I was expecting for a second time. And nine months later, on 29 November (a Saturday again!), I gave birth to our second son, Stephen. But this time, after my six weeks was up, I knew I had to return to work and there was only one convenient option.

'I'll go and see the manager at Friendship,' I told Jack.

John was now old enough to go to primary school and a local childminder would watch Stephen. So, the next day I went to see the manager. I still got a shudder as I walked through the iron gates and the noise of the shed hit me. Apart from the starting hours being 7.30am and a different manager, nothing, from what I could see, had changed and it was just how I'd remembered it. Conditions had not improved and everyone was still buying their dinner from the bakery.

'You can work on two looms,' he said (he was called Tommy and he was little and skinny).

'OK,' I replied.

The next day I woke with a familiar dread as I got John and Stephen ready before dropping them both off at the childminder.

'Here you go,' I said, passing her some butter as I left. 'In case you haven't got enough for the children.'

Now, the war may have been over but rationing wasn't and, in fact, for some products, it went on for 10 more years.

Heading for the mill, my aim was just to keep my head down and get on with work. As I've said before, I wasn't there to make friends or socialise. But, when Tommy took me back into the shed (still the same) and showed me my looms, suddenly this woman walked in and stood opposite my loom – we were beam to beam.

'Hello,' she said.

'I *love* your hair!' I gasped. 'I'm going to get my colour done like you.'

'Thanks,' she giggled.

For the first time, someone in the mill had actually made an impression on me. She had this amazing, plum-coloured hair and I thought it was the best thing since sliced bread. Her hair was shoulder-length, with loose curls, and it looked fantastic.

We got chatting (well, as much as we could before the looms started up!), but over the next few days we chatted on and off and I found out she was from Sabden and about the same age as me, though not married.

'I've met a lovely friend,' I told Jack back home. 'And I want my hair coloured plum!'

I never spoke to him about work and this was probably the first person I'd ever mentioned.

'I'm pleased there is someone in there you like,' he told me.

It was true and she was lovely. My only

regret now is that I can't, for the life of me, remember her name. It's funny, isn't it, how life works like that? Those you like, you struggle to remember, and yet I have no problem remembering my manager Tommy's name and I wasn't even that fussed about him.

Anyhow, it was a pleasure to work next to, let's say for argument's sake, Dorothy. And I always wondered how she got into work from Sabden, a village just a few miles from Read, nestled in Pendle Hill, because I was sure at that time there were no buses to and from there into Read. Thinking back, it's odd that I never asked her, but at the time I just never thought to.

We chatted mainly just in the morning first thing or as we clocked off, as we didn't get a brew in the sheds and at dinnertime I always went home as I had the tea to prepare and always made up the fire so it was all ready when everyone came home. But it was nice working alongside someone I liked, and it did make my day that bit more pleasant.

Most Monday mornings when I told her I'd just been at home with Jack and the boys, she'd tell me how she'd been out socialising.

'I went into Burnley for a few drinks,' she said.

'I don't blame you,' I told her. 'At least one of us has a social life!'

She was like a breath of fresh air.

We'd talk about clothes and shopping: 'I treated myself to a new coat,' I told her. 'It's red.' The style those days was double-breasted and this particular coat went down to my ankles.

'Sounds lovely,' she said.

But, when our council house on Green-acres was ready and we moved in when Stephen was five months old in April 1954, it was the hot topic of conversation.

'Is it nice?' asked Dorothy (she knew we'd been staying with Mum).

'Ooh *yes!*' I said. 'I'm just grateful for our own house and more space.'

The semi-detached had three bedrooms and a bathroom. I was pleased to be back living in Read, and working opposite Dorothy did make it slightly more bearable, but still my heart wasn't in it and, if I could have left, I would.

As the years went by, I still disliked the mill and just focused on my purpose for being there but at least it was nice having a friend. And, even though I didn't like the mill, it didn't stop me being conscientious. I've always been a hard worker and, although I didn't like the job, that didn't mean I didn't give it my all. To me, if I was doing it, then everything had to be right. I had to keep making sure everything was right; the cloth must be perfect.

So, because of that, I was always on pins in case I'd missed an end (something wrong with your cloth) and would wait with worry after I'd taken my cloth for inspection. Once you'd taken it off your loom, you carried it on a trolley into the warehouse and returned to your looms while the overlookers (men who checked your cloth) checked it. And, if it was wrong, then someone from the warehouse would come and get you. I'd be on pins until the next day and if no one had come for me by then, I knew my cloth was fine.

'Go, get her off number seven,' they'd instruct (they knew who everyone was because your loom had a number on it). So, my heart would be in my mouth as the lad from the warehouse walked through the shed. It was so humiliating if he came to you, as it meant everyone in the shed knew you'd done something wrong and consequently you lost money. Thankfully, it only happened once or twice to me but, when it did, I was shaking like a leaf.

'Oh, God, what have I done?' I asked, my heart sinking as I followed him to the warehouse.

'You left tail end of thread on so it's no good,' explained the overlooker. 'Don't let it happen again.'

But they didn't shout at us, and in fairness were pretty good. It was more that you were mad at yourself for letting it happen – and the shame of everyone else knowing.

'OK,' I muttered, before scurrying back to my looms.

I always thought there must be better weavers than me as there were some who worked there in the shed with me and I never saw them get called in. But, although this was something I dreaded about the mill, there was not one thing that would have forced me to leave without having another job. However, when Stephen turned three and became ill, that changed my perspective and I just wanted to quit.

The year was 1957 and kids were being given the vaccine jabs to protect them against polio. I was dead set against Stephen or John being vaccinated but was talked into it by a specialist at Burnley. I couldn't make up my mind but the specialist told me he thought I should let them have the vaccine because polio was going around Burnley at the time. So I went down to the doctor and agreed they could both have it.

At the time they were fine, but a week later Stephen was really poorly.

'I'm taking him to the doctors,' I told my mum. 'I think he's got polio.'

'Don't talk utter rubbish,' she said.

I could understand that; after all, the vaccine was supposed to prevent this from happening. But, unconvinced, I still took him as

I knew he wasn't right. He looked as if he only had a cold but his arm and head were droopy as though he was paralysed; he was also clingy and didn't want me to go to work.

'Just go, I'll watch him,' insisted Jack. He was off sick so there was no point in us both being off.

'OK,' I agreed, unconvinced.

Before I headed to the mill, I went to see my doctor, described the symptoms and he gave me some medicine for him to take and said he'd be up to see him the next day. Back home at lunchtime, Jack said Stephen hadn't eaten anything, he wouldn't even have orange juice.

Just then, two doctors arrived.

'I told you it was polio,' I said to Jack once the doctors had left. Doctors didn't just turn up on your doorstep, unannounced, for no reason.

The doctors told us they thought it was polio and they wanted to get Stephen to hospital just in case; I was so relieved. En route, he started screaming and I'll never forget the smell – it was like meat going off.

Stephen was in the Marsden Cross Fever Hospital in Burnley for four weeks. Jack and me took it in turns to be with him and, when he was eventually OK to come home, I went back to work. Tommy the manager was great and so was everyone else in the mill. Despite what I thought of the place, they were good with me when it mattered and I appreciated that. But the following day I walked out of the mill at lunchtime to find John standing at the gates.

'What are you doing?' I asked as I rushed towards him.

'They've closed the school,' he told me (he would have been seven at the time). 'They said we had to go home.'

I heard they put new toilets in and soon after our house was fumigated, following the confirmation that Stephen had had polio. And I was convinced he must have caught it from the vaccine. He became ill 10 days after the first injection and was supposed to have two more, which I never allowed him or John to have. But people in the village obviously thought the same as me; some even started to give me a wide berth.

'I've seen people walking towards me then cross the street,' I fumed to Jack. 'It's like they think they can catch it from me!'

I couldn't believe people in my own village could behave like that and be so bigoted. In fairness, no one at work was like that.

'That's it,' I said. 'I'm not working *and* living in this village!'

Something had to give so I went to Longsworth Mill, where our Marjorie, and now our Joyce too, worked, to see if there were any jobs. And a few days later, I handed in my notice at Friendship.

'Any time you want a job, there is one for you,' Tommy told me.

Although I had no intention of returning, I was chuffed he had said that, as he needn't have done so. And when my neighbour, who also worked at the mill, told me that the manager had been sorry to lose me, I was even more chuffed.

'Aye,' he said 'if all the workers in there were as conscientious as you then it'd be the happiest weaving shed around,' he added.

I didn't have anything like a leaving do, and I didn't even have any drinks or a collection. I'm not sure if it was because of lack of money, or the fact that I wasn't that well known, but I wasn't bothered. And, in fairness, a few did wish me well. But I was sorry to say so long to Dorothy.

'I'm sad to see you go,' she told me.

'I know, I'll miss you too,' I replied. 'Look after yourself.'

I liked Dorothy but we didn't keep in touch. It wasn't something you did back then; I was busy working, as well as being a mum and wife. Anyhow, she wanted different things to me, being single. But even now, all these years later, I still cherish that friendship – and gasp in awe at her wonderful hair!

Days later, I started at Longsworth Mill in Whalley. Actually called Judge Walmsley

174

Mill, it was located at the end of Longsworth Road, in Billington, so it was known as Longsworth Mill. It closed in 1966 and is now occupied by Harrison Engineering. They put on a special bus from Read at 7.10am and it got you there just in time for the 7.30am start. On the bus with me were our Joyce and a nice couple who both worked at the mill – he was a tackler and she was a weaver.

The conditions in there were the same but, here, they had duckboards down and everything was powered by steam. But the one thing I noticed more was how friendly everyone was. And no sooner had I started up my looms than someone came round and asked if I wanted to put in for the day trip to Blackpool.

'Are you interested?' asked the woman.

'Er, I'm not sure,' I replied. I'd been used to keeping myself to myself but, also in Friendship, I'd never been asked on a day trip.

'Go on!' said Linda, my next-door neighbour who worked there. 'It's a good giggle.'

She was about the same age as me, married, but didn't have children. Like I said before, I didn't often click with people but with Linda I did. Of course, I knew her anyway, but working alongside her in the mill we became the best of friends.

'You fancy a drink in Burnley this weekend?' she asked me.

'Ooh, why not?' I smiled. 'Let me check with Jack first.'

As well as Linda, I got friendly with an older lady called Mrs Cliff. She kind of took me under her wing and used to help me.

'Oh, no!' I sighed, if my end dropped off.

'Not to worry, love,' she'd say, leaving her loom and coming over to help. 'Here's what you should do.'

'Thank you,' I smiled.

Everyone was so friendly in the mill and, while I still didn't like the actual job, I was beginning to see the appeal of the mills. But a couple of years later, when Lucas Engineering got back in touch with me, I didn't have to think twice.

'I'm leaving,' I told Linda and Mrs Cliff.

I didn't have a leaving do or whip round, as no one had any money to do that, but Mrs Cliff bought me an ornamental jug.

'Thank you,' I choked.

I wasn't sad to leave the mill but I was sorry to leave the people I'd met because they were a good bunch in there. And I had to admit that Dad's words had served me well over the years and kept me working. Knowing I'd never have to weave again was the best feeling in the world, though!

I went on to work at Lucas Engineering for another 30 years. Once I'd left Longsworth, I really didn't give the mills a second thought. When I heard about the threat of closures, I felt sorry for those workers who didn't have any other means of making a living, but that was all. And when I learned that Friendship, Queen's and Longsworth had finally closed, I was sorry for the remaining workers but I'm pleased my sons never had to work there. I'm not doing down the mills but I always wanted better for my family.

Both my sons got married and I became a grandmother to six, and great-grandmother to nine children. Sadly, I lost my Jack in 1989, so in 2004 I moved to Clitheroe. But, as lives go, I don't think I can grumble as I've had a good one.

'I'm going in mill,' I told Dad one tea-time. His face dropped. 'Really?' he said. 'Muriel likes it,' I replied. 'She's a beamer. Will you ask for me to do the same?' After a few seconds' silence, he replied, 'Aye, if that's what you want.' A couple of days later, he came back with some news: the manager had said that I could start immediately. I was so excited.

Part Three:

Marjorie Wilkinson

CHAPTER NINE

Reality of the Mill

Shovelling down my bacon and eggs, I couldn't wait to get a move on.

'Someone's keen,' Mum smiled, clearing away my plate.

'Can we go?' I asked Dad, who was sitting beside me at the table in our living room.

Rolling his eyes, he took a sip of his brew and stood up. 'Come on then,' he sighed.

Unlike me, Dad wasn't in a hurry to get to work! But today, in August 1934, it was my first day at Stonebridge Manufacturing Company Ltd., a cotton mill in Chatburn, and I couldn't wait to get started. And right on cue, the familiar sound boomed through the village.

'Come on,' I urged. 'We'll be late!'

Every morning, at 6.40am, a loud blower resembling a ship's horn sounded from the mill to make sure any workers who were still in bed were up. Every day bar Sunday it went off, and it was so loud you could hear it across the whole village. Can you imagine doing that today? It just wouldn't happen, but, back then, no one thought anything of it, although I always felt sorry for those folk on Ribble Lane, right next to the mill. I know it never went off at the end of the day but I'm struggling to remember whether it ever went off at 1.20pm to signal the end of dinner. I just know it went off in the morning to stop the workers sleeping in and, when they used to start work at 6am, it went off even earlier: an hour before, at 5.40am. I'd heard it so many times before, but today it was different.

Today, it meant something.

'You'll not be as keen in a day or two,' Dad smirked, shaking his head.

But I wasn't having any of it. My friend Muriel had told me about the mill and I couldn't wait to get in it.

Almost 80 years later, as a 93-year-old lady, it's funny thinking back to the young, naïve girl I was then. I worked in there for 45 years and, trust me, my enthusiasm never lasted that long! But I have fond memories of the mill, including family, friendship and love – especially meeting my husband. I also wanted to let people know what happened and give them an insight into what working life was really like, back then.

It's so different from today. I don't think some people, especially the younger ones, would be able to comprehend it. In those days, you were just relieved and glad to get a job (and keep it) that you'd never think about leaving. Whereas today, if workers aren't happy, for whatever reason, they leave and find a new job or claim benefits – the two choices we never had. There wasn't the variety of jobs when I was 14 years old and leaving school, so the mill was the obvious choice, living in Chatburn. It was a good source of employment, especially for our village, but today people wouldn't put up with the conditions. Yet, oddly enough, I didn't think they were that bad at the time. It's only now when I reflect back on it and compare it to the modern world that I see how some things wouldn't be allowed today. I also think we've gone too far the other way now. For example, in my last week in the mill before I retired at 59, we got a canteen and one of the lady workers was asked if she'd shift jobs and work in there instead. That wouldn't happen today, but back then people rallied round and, if you suddenly shifted jobs, you just accepted it and did it. Today, they'd either pack it in or there are so many rules and regulations the manager wouldn't be able to do it. But back then you didn't bother as you were just thankful to have a job – regardless of how much you disliked it. However, you probably won't be able to begin to understand what I mean, until I explain a bit more about what it was like working in the mill, but, to get a taste of who I am and what my life was like, I thought it best to start from the beginning.

I was born Marjorie Barnes on 15 April 1920 to William Barnes and Jane Hitchen. We lived at 72 St Paul's Street, in Low Moor, an area of Clitheroe in Lancashire, a market town in the borough of the Ribble Valley and home to Clitheroe Castle, believed to be one of the smallest Norman keeps in the country. At that time, Clitheroe was the same as the rest of the country in that it was in Depression with real poverty. Men had returned home from the Great War expecting life to be wonderful, only to find they had no jobs to return to and were instead forced to experience the long queues at the Employment Exchange. The only slight advantage to living in Clitheroe was that coal was readily available to heat homes and home-grown vegetables could be produced in the summer months to supplement what food could be bought, but it was still a difficult time. Then, Clitheroe had a population of 11,000 and the biggest employers in the town were the 15 cotton mills; other large employers were grain mills, bobbin mills, bleaching and quarrying.

Low Moor had been purpose-built for the workers of the cotton mill, Thomas Garnett & Sons. In 1900, the mill had been there for 200 years; it employed around 700 workers and had 1,160 looms.

I couldn't begin to tell you how my parents met or their ages when they married and started a family. The only thing I know is that they were both from Low Moor and worked in the mill. Now, with sharing my story and thinking back over my life, that's something I wish I knew. In fact, I wish I'd asked about lots of things but, in those days, you didn't think the same as we do today. We weren't so forward as the youngsters are now and we didn't ask questions the same as they do.

So, it's my guessing that they either met because they lived in the same area or it was through the mill. Dad was a weaver and Mum a winder, and I do know they both had to do the half-timer system. That meant they had to do a half day at school and the other half at the mill before they left school altogether. The system was only abolished in 1918, but not fully implemented in Lancashire until 1921.

Dad was tallish, with thin, dark hair. A nice fella, he was a good father and husband. He didn't drink or smoke and all his money went on his family. Mum was small, with long dark hair, which was permed and worn in plaits and tied up around her head, a popular style then. She was fairly quiet but nice natured and could be a bit of fun. I was never scared of Mum or Dad – they were both caring and never raised a hand to me.

I only ever remember getting told off as any child would.

I had an older brother called Edgar, who was 12 when I was born. Because of the age gap, I didn't really have that much to do with him but I know he was at the Clitheroe Grammar School when I came along. At some point, Mum had given up working in the mills to be a mother and housewife, but I'm not sure if she'd gone back to work in between having Edgar and me or had never gone back since having my older brother.

We lived in our two up, two down and when I was about four years old my brother, Robert Ernest, was born. I don't recall Mum being pregnant or the details of him being a baby but, when I got a bit older, I remember thinking I liked having a young brother. Around this time, I started at Low Moor Primary School and, although the memory of my younger years is sketchy, one thing I do remember is being happy and content.

Like most people, we didn't have a lot of money but we weren't poor either. Mum and Dad were very careful how they spent their earnings and we were well looked after. As I've said, Dad didn't drink (or gamble either) and I don't remember him ever going out socialising. His life was for his family so all the money he brought in was spent on us. We always had three good meals and tea-time was something hearty, like potato pie, vegetables and a sweet. We wore nice clothes and I was lucky that I never needed to have second-hand ones. I remember Mother taking me to a clothes shop in Low Moor, which sold ladies' fashion. I'm afraid I can't remember the name, but I know a lady owned it and, if we didn't go there, we'd go to shops in Clitheroe. And back then, everyone wore hats all the time – especially on a Sunday – so Mother would take me to a clothing shop in Clitheroe. The name Coleman's Clothing springs to mind but I can't be certain that's the right name or even spelled like that, but what I do remember are the shop windows: they were full of hats, many of them shaped like plant pots!

I had a good relationship with Mum and Dad, but I never did as much with them as kids do today with their parents. Mum wasn't overly tactile, but, when I was ill, she would give me cuddles and I always knew I was well loved by them both. They instilled good manners in my brothers and me (although, by then, Edgar was married and had left home). But I was never expected to do any chores at this age. I was able to have fun as a child as I played out on the street or in the fields for hours, and the farmer would just leave us to it! At weekends, Mum and Dad would take Robert and me for picnics in the nearby fields or down the river.

In January 1928 we moved to Victoria Avenue, in Chatburn – a village next to Clitheroe – because Dad had a job at Stonebridge Manufacturing Company. I was only eight at the time so I don't remember much but I was told that we were moving as Dad had a new job. Despite Thomas Garnett & Sons being one of the largest spinning and manufacturing mills in Lancashire, the slump in the cotton trade had hit hard for it closed down that year.

Thinking back, Dad was lucky to get another job. And because he'd always worked in the mill, I always knew about it in the sense that was where he worked, but obviously, at this tender age, I didn't really understand much about what went on inside. As a child I'd walked past it, and when we moved to Chatburn I heard the blower going every morning.

'What's that noise?' I asked, the first morning I heard it.

'It's to let Dad knows he needs to get to work,' said Mum.

Other times, if I walked past the mill, I'd hear how noisy the weaving sheds were but it was just a part of life as working in a mill was what everyone did. I suppose in the same sense as the factories that people work in now, children don't question it; that's just how it is.

It was only when I got older that I realised

how much Dad hated it, as I never heard him moan once when I was growing up. The odd times he would say how loud it was and that he got dirty, but that was all. But the older I got and the more aware I became, I realised the mill wasn't his choice and he'd never wanted to go in. He had been forced into it when really he wanted to do something with his hands, like be a carpenter or joiner, but his ambition was quashed by his family: 'If we've had to go in mill, so can our William,' his sisters told his parents. So, he'd had no choice. But, being the person he was, he knew he had to earn money and the mill was the only way he could make sure his family were taken care of – and we were. Compared to some children, I suppose we were quite lucky.

Our house was a two up, two down and one of the 100 houses that had been built by the mill for their workers. We paid rent – sadly, I haven't a clue how much. Since we didn't have a bathroom, we used to wash in the sink and have a tin bath in front of the fire once a week; hot water was provided through the geyser. Ours was white and above our sink; I suppose it was a bit similar to boilers today, but it had a metal tube that the water ran out of. We had two nice rooms downstairs, and a kitchen, and we had two upstairs bedrooms and an attic. In the front room (the best room) we had a three-piece suite and a sewing machine. Our living room had two fireside chairs, a table, sideboard and an organ, on which my mum would play hymns at night. In the kitchen there was a sink, cooker and table, but we always ate in the living room as the kitchen was smaller. Then, out the back door, four steps led down to the yard and the outside toilet.

We had nice bedroom furniture, too, which a lot of people may not have had back then. In my parents' room, Dad had made a wooden bedroom suite, which was a chest of drawers, a dressing table (and mirror) and wardrobe. It just went to show that he was capable of much more than the mill and given the chance he would have made a success of being a carpenter or joiner.

I switched schools to Chatburn Primary, just down the road from our house. I used to wear a jumper, grey skirt with a pleat in to my knee, knee socks and little pump-style shoes with a strap across. In the summer I would just wear a cotton summer dress.

As in Low Moor, I used to go and play out in the fields for hours on end and, of course, every Sunday we would put on our Sunday best and head to Chatburn Methodist Church (any socialising we did was with the church). Mum always looked smart in a hat and I'd wear my best dress and coat.

'Go and change into your old dress,' Mum

would say the minute we got back into the house. 'They're only for best.' And even to this day I still do the same thing! The minute I'm back home, I get out of my 'best' clothes and put on something else.

I used to enjoy school, and back then kids would stay at primary school until they left at 14, so I was excited to be one of the first pupils to start at Ribblesdale Senior School in Clitheroe – now known as Ribblesdale High School – when it was opened in August 1932 by HRH The Princess Royal. Ribblesdale and Pendle Primary School had been built at the same time, so they opened together.

'It's so big!' I told Mum and Dad. 'Two-storey, with four classrooms!' And nowadays, of course, it is even bigger. Back then, we didn't have a uniform unlike the pupils today, so I just wore my usual skirt and jumper. I enjoyed the lessons and, if memory serves me right, academically, I was about average. I remember taking exams in English, Maths and History.

At school, I became pals with a girl called Muriel Ridley. She was a pretty, plump girl with dark hair and she lived in Chatburn, too, so we caught the bus together. I remember in December 1933 I was a bit sad when Muriel was due to finish at the end of term because she'd turned 14. Once you reached that age, you had to leave at the end of the next term.

By then, because I was older, I was more aware of Dad's job and I knew how much he hated the mill. He'd supported our Edgar when he said he wanted to be a confectioner and always told Robert and me how he wanted more for us: 'I don't want you to go in,' he'd say. I never really asked why, but, looking back and knowing what I do now, I think he just wanted something better for us. But I never quizzed him on the actual job or the conditions; I think it was more the fact that he wanted to be a carpenter or joiner and I don't think he wanted us to suffer the same fate that he himself had. Instead, he wanted us to do something we actually wanted to do. In fact, he got his wish with Edgar and later with Robert, who started at Sowerbutts Furniture in Clitheroe (still in business today) as a carpet layer when he left school. Mum never said anything but I knew she was happiest being a housewife and didn't miss the mill. But in January 1934, when I met Muriel and she was raving about the mill, all Dad's concerns went out of my head.

'I'm a beamer and it's really good,' she grinned. 'It's a big room but I work with some nice girls my age, and we manage to have a gossip and a giggle. And it's not noisy, like the sheds.' Muriel explained that the job of a beamer is to wind the warp from

194

the bobbins of cotton and fix them onto the beam, which is a heavy lump of wood, like a huge bobbin, ready for weaving.

'It sounds good,' I said.

I couldn't understand why Dad didn't like it.

So, as the months ticked down to April that same year and my school leaving date edged closer, I began thinking about work. It wasn't like today, with high expectations, as there wasn't a big importance placed on a woman's job. I think I did a couple of exams in Maths and English but I couldn't tell you what result I got, although I'm sure it was about average. But that didn't make any difference to my job: the only opportunities available to me were a sewing place in Clitheroe or the mill. Well, it made sense to go in the mill, despite Dad's thoughts. Not only would it mean I wouldn't have to travel, but, after what Muriel had said, it sounded like it was a good place to work and now I wanted to go in! I often wonder, had she not been so positive about her experience inside the mill, would I have listened to Dad and found something else? But I suppose I'll never know. After all, I was young and impressionable.

'I'm going in mill,' I told Dad one tea-time.

His face dropped. *'Really?'* he said.

'Muriel likes it,' I replied. 'She's a beamer.

195

Will you ask for me to do the same?'

After a few seconds' silence, he replied, 'Aye, if that's what you want.'

A couple of days later, he came back with some news: the manager had said that I could start immediately. I was so excited.

'You'll be paid eight shillings and five pence,' said Dad (that would be about £1 in today's money).

From Dad working there, I already knew the working hours were 7am to 8.30am, then half an hour for breakfast, then 9am to 12.35pm and an hour for dinner, and finish at 5.10pm. I never knew why it was those queer hours, especially the finishing time. Over the years, I've often wondered if there was a reason for them and my only conclusion is that the hours revolved around the train times. Back then, you could catch a train from Chatburn to Clitheroe, but this service was closed in 1962 under the Beeching Cuts (also known as the Beeching Axe). The Beeching Cuts was the mass closure of railways and local services across Great Britain with the aim of restructuring and reducing the route networks. Consequently, Clitheroe and Chatburn were just two of the stations affected (Clitheroe reopened as a passenger service in May 1994).

So, a couple of days later, I finished school and on the Monday morning I was an eager beaver, ready to get started.

'All set?' I asked Dad.

Usually he came home for his bacon and eggs in the breakfast break but today, on my first day, Mum thought it best that I start the day with a full belly.

'Have a nice day,' Mum smiled, as Dad and me walked out onto the street heading towards the mill.

My face was free of make-up (no one wore it in the mill) and over my jumper and skirt I wore a light-blue overall, a bit like a tabard. To this day, I can't remember what we chatted about, if we did at all. I just remember a lot of workers heading in the same direction! And as we walked down Ribble Lane, and the big square building came into view, my stomach knotted with apprehension and excitement.

The mill consisted of four weaving sheds: two big ones and two smaller ones, which were all on the ground floor and opposite a three-storey building, which I later found out housed the warehouse, then the warps and the winding room (where I was going to be) on the top floor.

'I'll take you to the office,' said Dad, leading me through the warehouse and up the stairs to the third floor. Now, I'd been past the mill a hundred times but I couldn't believe how big it was! 'Just wait here,' Dad told me before he nipped inside.

Minutes later, a chap from the office told

me to follow him. It wasn't the manager, Mr Conyers, as I knew from what Dad had said he was an older chap.

'I'll see you at home for dinner,' said Dad.

I followed this chap, who led me through to the end of the winding room. In there were a number of frames, a good few metres long, and the winding machines were used to wind yarn from cops, which was a bobbin of thread used to either warp or weft onto bobbins. I thought I might have seen Muriel, but it was such a big room!

I was led to the corner of the room, where three other girls about my age were standing.

'You'll be doffing for time being before we can train you to beam,' the chap told me.

Doffing means to doff, or take off, the full bobbins and replace them with the empty ones. In fact, that's where the term 'to doff your hat' derives from.

'Oh, right,' I said, trying not to sound too disappointed. After all, I was just grateful to have a job – the last thing I'd ever do would be answer back or moan.

'So, stand here and, when one of the winders shouts, "I need help", you run to them and take off their full bobbins and replace – the lot, if needed.'

The winders wound the bobbins for the weft – the job Mum used to do. I'm struggling to remember the other girls' names but they were pleasant enough. I don't think we chatted much, though – I was too busy concentrating in case someone shouted out!

Before I knew it, it was time for dinner. With only an hour, I dashed out of the mill and up the road back home. Once there, Dad was already sat down at the table in the living room as Mum served up a cooked dinner.

'Well?' asked Mum, plating me up some.

'It's OK,' I replied, 'but I'm doffing, not beaming.'

'Oh, helping the winders?' said Mum fondly. She never talked about her days in the mill so this was rare – and quite nice to hear.

I nodded.

'I'm sure you'll be a beamer soon,' Dad reassured me, which meant a lot considering how he must have felt.

After shovelling down our meal, it was soon time to head back to the mill. I'm sure Dad and me chatted on our way back but I don't think it was about work. People didn't talk about it back then – even if it was your first day!

My week flew by and the odd time I saw Muriel we just had a quick chat, but that was all. So, by Saturday lunchtime when we finished at 11.45am and I had my first pay packet, I was ready to go and have some fun, so I went and found her.

'Fancy the pictures?' I asked, as we walked out.

'Reckon we deserve it after all that hard work!' she giggled. 'Do you like it then in there?'

To be honest, I wasn't sure what I thought at this stage as up to then I'd only been working with the girls doffing.

'Yeah, it's fine,' I replied. 'OK, meet you in an hour at the bus stop.'

I'd have to go home and have my dinner first and then we could catch the bus to Clitheroe. Back home, dinner was on the table and I handed Mum my wage.

'There you go,' she smiled, giving me something back. I can't remember how much but it was enough to go to the pictures and I didn't mind. Mum and Dad looked after me very well so I was happy to contribute to the housekeeping.

The weekend flew by and Monday morning was looming. This time, I walked down for 7am but, at 8.30am, Dad and I dashed back for breakfast.

'It's hard to eat it so quick,' I said, shovelling down the boiled egg Mum had made me.

But that's what everyone did, although I could never understand why we just didn't start a bit later and not have a breakfast break.

'You get used to it,' Dad smiled.

Before I knew it, I settled into a routine at work but I was still desperate to get beaming, especially when I saw Muriel and she used to tell me how well she got on with all the girls her age she worked with. So, finally, a few months later, I was delighted when the chap from the office told the four of us doffers we were going to be trained.

'You'll each have one week to learn,' he explained. 'Marjorie, follow me.'

I was going to be the first one to train, and so I followed him into a room where a tallish lady, wearing glasses, was waiting.

'Lizzie will train you for the first week,' he said, before leaving us.

'Hello,' she smiled. 'Your dad said you'd started.'

Lizzie was my mum's cousin and about the same age as her. She wasn't married and lived in Waddington, about four miles away. That was the thing about the mills – they were full of family or people you knew. Lizzie was so lovely I felt instantly at ease.

'Oh, hello,' I said. 'I'm glad you're doing it.'

At dinnertime, I went home and told Mum who was training me, and pleased it was someone I knew. And after a week our Lizzie told me I was picking it up quickly.

'*Really?*' I said.

'Yes,' she replied. 'You've really picked it

up. In fact, Mr Conyers even commented on it.'

'What did he say?' I asked.

'He said, "That Barnes lass seems to have taken to beaming, hasn't she?" So there!' she smiled.

So, when Lizzie told me I was moving to the big room to beam with 35 machines, I was made up. All I could think about was getting next to a group of girls my age and having the same good times as Muriel did.

My frame was a good size, perhaps a few metres, and I was to be working on the warp, which is the material that runs lengthways across the loom. It was like yards and yards of a rope but it was threaded and you'd call them 'threads' (but known as 'ends') and there'd be as many as 500 in the warp. We then had to put the warp on to a beam, and then this beam was for the labourer, who threaded the warp and set the loom up ready for weaving.

But as I stood before it my heart sank. It wasn't the prospect of standing all day in front of this huge piece of machinery – I was already used to that – it was the four women I'd been put with.

'Hello, love,' said one, introducing herself (I'm sorry to say that I can't, for the life of me, remember any of their names).

'Hello,' I replied.

'You'll be al'reet with us,' smiled another.

'And, if you need 'owt, just shout,' said another.

Don't get me wrong, they were all lovely and welcoming, but it was just the fact they were more my mum's age. All shapes and sizes, their faces were free of make-up and their hair was either in a short bob like mine or pinned up. Like me, they all wore an overall over their clothes. And unlike in the weaving sheds, we didn't have to lip read as it wasn't so noisy, just a general murmur. So, it was easier to chat and soon enough I'd found out they were all married, a couple had children and one was even a grandma. But while they told me about their families I just listened and smiled politely, but really I was so disappointed they weren't girls my own age.

At the time I don't think I admitted to anyone how disappointed I was; I certainly never told Mum and Dad. To be honest, after my first day in the mill I don't ever recall them asking me again how I was getting on, but back then you didn't – you just got on with it. It's only now, all these years later, when I'm thinking back that I remember how I felt. I'm not even sure if I ever told Muriel.

And as the days turned into weeks and the reality of the long hours and tiring days in the mill took hold, coupled with the fact I wasn't with girls my own age, it dawned on me that Dad had always been right – I should have done something else. But now, I was stuck: I'd made my bed so there was nothing more I could do but lie in it.

CHAPTER TEN

Settling In

Soon enough, I was in a routine of getting up, walking down to the mill, coming home for a quick breakfast and then back again for dinner, back to work and then home for tea. I think I'd built up this impression of what it would be like, ignoring my dad's concerns, and I soon realised how wrong I'd been. But I never heard any of the women I worked with moaning about it – they all just got their heads down and worked hard.

But before I knew it my first Christmas in the mill had arrived – and it was a very different affair to the holiday period we know and love today. Firstly, there was no tree and, if memory serves me right, I don't think there were even any paper trimmings and certainly no such thing as a party. I know later on, after the Second World War, we used to have a little party in our department and put up some paper trimmings, but that was a fair few years on, and again it wasn't arranged by the manager, but by us. So, this one day, it was nice when one of the women close to me suddenly broke out into the song 'Jingle Bells'.

And, with that, everyone joined in! As we all sang together, it felt so festive and really lifted my spirits. I was worried the manager would mind, but someone reassured me it would be fine.

The mill was good in that respect – they didn't mind you having a sing-a-long, so long as you kept hard at it while you did! I think that was the difference back then, as everyone grafted hard and the singing wasn't a chance to down tools and have a quick bunk off from working. It was actually something everyone could do together and was thoroughly appreciated by all. From then on, there wasn't a day went by before we finished on Christmas Eve when someone didn't break into a carol and everybody else joined in. In that respect, the mill was a great source of solidarity and it felt good to be part of it. And, thankfully, the manager never minded us singing. In fact, I rarely saw him; he only came into our room twice or perhaps three times a week, if that.

A family from Colne owned the mill but it was rare that we saw them, although we soon knew when they would be paying us a visit.

'Clean up,' said one of the women, 'we're getting a visit from bosses!'

The mill was founded by the Broughton family, who had mills in Colne, and when the father died he left it in the hands of his three sons. One died, but I remember Frank and Neville used to come over now and then, perhaps three times a year. I remember the first time I saw them; the pair walked past us all, dressed up in their posh suits, and never said a word – well, not to us mere workers, any road.

'They think we're beneath them, looking down at us,' said one of the women.

Over time, their sons and daughters took over and I remember the grandson being called John Berry and he was all right. But by then, I'm talking years later, when it was altogether different and because times had changed, he happily spoke to us, the workers, unlike his granddad.

Sorry, I've digressed a little. Anyhow, back to Christmas. So, we finished on Christmas Eve and we had Christmas Day and Boxing Day off. I have a feeling later on, we may have had Christmas Eve as a holiday but at that time I know we didn't. And, after Boxing Day, we had to go back to work and it was no more holidays until Easter, because at that time we didn't get New Year's Day off. It's funny now, thinking we had to work it, and, even though it wasn't the big celebration it is today, it was still awful having to go in. It was quite funny, though, because you'd see people dragging their heels (more than normal) into the mill, with some looking a bit worse for wear.

'Aye oop, he's had a good neet!' said one of the women next to me.

Giggling, I did feel a bit sorry for him!

Even though I'd spent that New Year's Eve at home with my family, like most people, thinking it didn't feel that much different to a normal night, there would still have been some who toasted the New Year in with far too much drink in the same way as some do today.

I may not have been at the mill that long but even I picked up on the general feeling that what the workers wanted was more holidays and better hours. I'd heard some departments had a union rep (I knew the weaving one did), but ours, the preparation department, didn't.

'What do they do?' I asked Dad.

'They help the common man,' he told me. 'They speak up on our behalf to get things better for us.'

Since the eighteenth century, the trade unions had been fighting for the workers' rights and privileges and there had been a long battle between the masters on the one side and the workers on the other. The 1919 Strike, which saw all cotton workers acting more or less in unison, had two main aims: to work a basic 48-hour week but be paid for overtime, and for the half-timer system to be abolished.

So, I'm not sure if someone suddenly decided or if we were just asked but I remember being told that two union reps from Nelson, a town about seven miles away, were coming over to hold a meeting upstairs in the local Black Bull pub.

'You should go,' said Dad.

'Why the pub?' I asked.

'Union rep in't allowed in mill,' he replied.

It must have been one night after work, as I walked there with the older women I worked with. When we arrived, the room was packed – at least 40-odd of us, plus some of the male tapers (they put the pattern into the yarn), I bet. There were these two men standing at the front. I couldn't tell you how old they were but they just looked and dressed like normal men, like my dad.

'We will do what we can for you,' said one. 'And, if you have any trouble, tell us and we'll fight it for you.' They talked about getting us less working hours for the same pay and better holiday (they called a meeting about once or twice a year if they had anything to tell us).

Eventually, we got our hours changed to 8am until 12.30pm and then 1.30pm until 5pm, with no Saturday mornings, but that didn't come into play until after the Second World War. And it wasn't until 1974 that New Year's Day became a bank holiday.

As time went on, I never really took to the job but it was a wage and I just had to get on with it. So, it helped when my wage went up after I'd been there for 12 months.

'Great!' I cried, as I ripped open my pay packet to see 12 shillings.

'It goes up after one year,' explained the office man, handing out the wages.

Well, I wasn't going to argue with that! I probably gave Mum more but she was always fair and made sure I had enough money for myself.

Now, although I was pleased with my new wage, I didn't know whether it was the same for men and women. I didn't think there was a difference but I could be wrong because, as I keep saying, I never asked. But I do know most of the workers were on piece work – getting paid for what they did – anyhow. To this day, I couldn't tell you what my dad earned but, from how we lived, he must have been a good worker.

And the first time I opened my pay packet and saw more money in it, I didn't know what it was.

'Holiday pay,' said the staff man.

'*Really?*' I gasped. I felt like jumping for joy, as I couldn't believe I was getting paid to go on my holiday! I can't remember how much it was at the time but, as the years went on, I'll never forget when I got my first five-pound note. I felt as rich as royalty.

'Fancy taking me out?' joked one of the men.

As I was young and naïve, sometimes the men in there would tease me.

'You got a boyfriend?' asked one, trying to make me blush.

'No,' I replied.

'Well, when you do, make sure he keeps his hands to himself!' he smirked.

But as my cheeks turned crimson I knew he was only teasing and soon it became regular banter. The more timid you were, the more the men would tease you – like everywhere, really – so I soon wised up. After all, they were really friendly and it was all harmless fun. In fact, it made the day go round that bit quicker.

As far as romances in the mill went, I never really knew of that many – although I met my husband there, which I'll come to later – but there would be gossip about certain people carrying on together, especially in the weaving shed!

'Have you heard about so and so?' one of the men would say. 'Getting up to all sorts in that shed!'

The weaving shed seemed to be the main place that people – single ones, that is – carried on. But it was all hearsay and gossip, and, after all, that's what makes the world turn round and your day go a bit quicker.

Anyhow, even if people were carrying on, it was nothing new and it still goes on today, I imagine, as people meeting and courting at work was nothing unusual.

Mainly the mill was full of good banter and mixed with families, though. Obviously, Dad worked in there but I knew other people where the mum, dad and granddad were all in there, too.

Although I was now becoming used to the mill, when the clock struck 11.45am on a Saturday, I was out of there! It was the best feeling in the world, knowing I didn't have to come back to the mill for a full day and a half. And, once I'd had a good dinner, I was ready to go out.

Now, there weren't any social activities to do with the mill and, because I worked with the older ladies (I say 'older', but I bet they were only in their 40s or 50s), it wasn't like I'd meet up with them so I tended to meet Muriel or go to Clitheroe and see my friend, Ida, whom I'd known since a girl from the village, but she moved to Clitheroe later. Or I'd have a walk around the town or the fields with my friends, or even Mum and Dad. And, of course, I still went to Methodist church every Sunday so that would be all morning and then Mum would cook dinner. Sometimes if there was anything social on at the church – say, on a Saturday – we'd do that, too. As a family we spent a lot of time there. To this day, I still go to the Methodist church every Sunday, and for 50 years I taught piano at the Sunday school and played in the church.

As the years ticked by, the mill was one of the biggest parts of my life but, every Monday morning, it was still an effort to get myself down there. I wasn't passionate about the job and the enthusiasm I'd had when I first started there was well gone! Although I got on well with the women, I still wished I worked with a younger crowd. So, this one Monday, when the manager told everyone in our department we could have a day off that week, I was over the moon. And considering how hard the weavers worked, it didn't seem fair that it was us who had the day off when they weren't even allowed a brew break during the day.

'Why?' I asked.

'Work has slowed down while we're waiting for the warps [thread which runs lengthways across the loom] to come in,' he explained, 'so take Wednesday off.'

Well, at the time I thought this was brilliant.

'Lie in for me, then!' I cried.

After that, it started to happen a bit more regularly, probably about once or twice a month. We either had a day off or started at 9am and we skipped breakfast. So, on our days off, Muriel and I would go to the pictures or have a walk around the fields.

'This is great,' she said. 'They're all hard at it and we're out here!'

But what hadn't registered in our minds at the time was that fewer hours meant fewer pennies. And, when my wage packet didn't have the usual 12 shillings, I wasn't happy.

Oh, no! This is no good, I sighed to myself.

But, while we were worrying about our pay packets, something far greater was causing a stir, not just among the mill workers but the whole country too: the threat of war. It was April 1939 and the Second World War was looming; it was all everybody was talking about in the mill. We knew that Hitler wanted to dominate Europe and he had already taken control of Austria and Czechoslovakia. Obviously, there was no television in those days but we kept up to date as much as possible with the wireless.

I remember seeing a picture of our Prime Minister, Neville Chamberlain, waving a piece of paper after going to visit Hitler and saying there'd be no war. But, sadly, that was never to be.

On 3 September 1939, as we all went to the Methodist church as we did every Sunday morning, I never thought this would be a day to change all our lives. I think the service must have been coming to the end when a man suddenly ran in.

'We're going to war!' he announced. 'It's just been on the wireless.'

Now, although I can remember hearing those words, I couldn't tell you who had said them or what the minister said after that. To be honest, while it wasn't something we wanted to happen, I think everyone knew it was coming.

The atmosphere shifted. Once home we sat in the living room and switched on the wireless. Our Prime Minister, Neville Chamberlain, had announced the news at 11.15am in a broadcast on the BBC lasting 12 minutes and 38 seconds, which he started off by saying: 'I am speaking to you from the Cabinet Room at 10 Downing Street. This morning, the British Ambassador in Berlin handed the German government a final note stating that unless we heard from them by 11 o'clock that they were prepared at once to withdraw their troops from Poland a state of war would exist between us. I have to tell you now that no such undertaking has been received and consequently this country is at war with Germany.'

Once the Prime Minister had finished, this was followed by government announcements telling us how we should carry on and how the war would affect our lives. For example, we were told that places of entertainment, like theatres and cinemas, would be closed until further notice because, if they were hit by a bomb, large numbers would be killed or injured; we were also instructed to carry our gas masks everywhere and to keep off the streets as much as possible. The different sounds during an air raid were explained, too: hand rattles were used to warn of poisonous gas and hand bells to signal there was no danger, while a two-minute siren on the same note signalled you could leave the air raid shelter.

One thing that happened in Chatburn was the mill hooter sounding. I'm not sure why, but it never went off during the war. And do you know, if memory serves me, I'm sure it was never used again.

Funnily enough, I don't remember feeling frightened. I mean, out in the rural sticks as we were, we didn't seem in as much danger as, say, in a city. To be honest, the fear was more around the husbands and sons who'd have to fight.

'Just take note of what they said,' Dad told us. 'Just be careful.'

'Will do,' Robert and me said.

I was 19 years old when war broke out, and we all felt awful. The only relief for us as a family (especially my parents) was that Robert was only 15 and therefore too young to sign up and my father, who had served in the First World War, didn't need to fight either (I'm not sure if this was down to his age or his health). I could see how terrible it was, especially for my parents, but the news was also tinged with some relief.

'I'm sure it'll be over by Christmas,' said Mum. That was the general consensus but, sadly, we soon found out it wasn't the case.

The next day in the mill, there was a sombre atmosphere. Again, everyone thought the war would only last a few months so they tried to stay positive, but it was difficult, especially as most people in the mill knew someone whose son or husband would be called up.

'It's awful,' said one of the women. 'She has two sons that have to go.'

'And that lass in weaving, she's not long married and he'll be called,' added another.

Similar sentiments echoed around the building for weeks but, apart from worry for the men and those left behind, there wasn't a sudden sense of fear.

'We'll be al'reet here,' said one of the men. 'It's the cities that will get bombed.'

But, sadly, this wasn't the case.

CHAPTER ELEVEN

War

Wednesday, 30 October 1940 started off no different to any other day. I'd just nipped home for dinner and I was on my way back to work for the afternoon. Grabbing my coat, I headed out the door and towards the mill.

Since the war had started, as I mentioned earlier, we'd been given gas masks and told to carry them around with us at all times. I can't even remember who distributed them or how we got them – just how horrible they looked. We were also instructed to get blackout curtains, although I couldn't tell you where from, which we had to make sure were drawn every night, and, if you heard a knock at your door, it was more than likely the air raid warden who patrolled the streets nightly had come to tell you off for leaving a gap in your curtain.

I can't remember how many times the siren went off but it seemed to be quite frequent, although I don't ever recall feeling *that* scared. At first, we carried our gas masks everywhere but after a while I got a little complacent and sometimes forgot mine. I suppose, because of where we lived, I never really felt we were in danger of being bombed. And on that particular day I can't remember whether or not I was carrying my mask, but I don't think I was.

The war had little consequence as far as how I felt about the mill was concerned. Among the workers, the daily talk was about the war and if anyone heard any news of a local casualty or death we'd be told. Everyone rallied round and I suppose by now I was used to being in the mill so I didn't give it much thought. But one thing that bothered me more was that the days off we were given were becoming more frequent, especially now during wartime. It might have suited those married women who could do an extra day's cleaning but it was no good for Muriel and me.

'I'm sick of it,' I told her as we walked back into the mill together. 'I think we should head to the Labour Exchange on our next day off and see what we can volunteer for.'

'Good idea,' she replied, as we climbed the steps of the mill to the top floor before going to other ends of the room.

'See you later,' I said.

Soon, everyone was hard at it, and I think it was about half an hour later when suddenly we heard a loud crack and the glass panels from the ceiling began to fall down on us. As a few screams and a sense of panic filled the air, on instinct I crouched down and backed myself up against the wall. It happened so fast I couldn't tell you where the other women were, or if they'd done the same – all I could see was shards of glass sprayed across the stone floor.

My mind raced, but at that point I didn't have a clue what had happened. Being bombed was the obvious answer, but we'd not heard any explosion and there'd been no warning siren so surely it couldn't have been us? Besides, why would they bomb Chatburn? It wasn't as if we had barracks here or we were a city. But, as more pieces of glass fell, I knew, whatever had caused it, the main thing was to get out. For all I knew, the entire ceiling could have collapsed at any point. Suddenly, one of the men started shouting for us all to leave.

'We have to evacuate, come on!' he yelled.

As I dashed across the room towards the stairs and joined the rest of the workers scrambling to get out, thankfully, it didn't look as if anyone was seriously hurt. There were a few women holding their arms as though they'd been hit and some clothes were splattered with specks of blood, but no one seemed injured. As I raced down the stairs, Dad came charging up.

'Are you all right?' he said.

'Yes,' I panted, 'just a little shook up as the

glass started coming in.'

'You need to get out,' he ordered.

As Dad followed me back down the stairs, he told me they thought it was a bomb.

'*Really?*' I gasped. 'In the village?'

'They think it's hit one of the houses and the effect of the blast has caused the glass to shatter,' he explained. 'But we need to get everyone out – quickly.'

When we reached the ground floor, instead of going out up Ribble Lane as usual, we went out the back way and through the fields. It wasn't safe to go back up Ribble Lane because of the destruction and debris.

'Go straight home,' instructed Dad.

He and the other male workers stayed behind to help clean up the factory and get the roof repaired. Meanwhile, the women trekked across the field in silence. I think we were all shocked and frightened to death that the reality of war had touched our sleepy village. The minute I walked through the front door, Mum flung her arms around me.

'I've been so worried,' she said. 'Are you all right?'

'Yes,' I replied. 'No one really knew what was happening.'

'I saw it,' she said (she'd been looking after Kenneth, Edgar's son). 'I was in the yard and holding Kenneth, and I looked up and the plane was there. The minute I saw the swastika on the side, I dashed back indoors and went under the stairs. I couldn't believe he was so close, it was quite terrifying.'

And I knew it must have been – I mean, who expects to see an enemy plane that close?

'Dad has stayed at the mill to help clean up,' I told her. Suddenly, I got a little teary-eyed: 'I was never frightened of the war before,' I choked.

Mum gave me a cuddle. 'You're safe now,' she soothed.

Hours later, Dad returned home. He told us that two bombs had been dropped and news had spread around the village that there had been casualties – and deaths.

'A Miss Alice Robinson's house took a direct hit and she has been taken to hospital,' said Dad. 'I'm sorry to say that a lady called Mrs Elizabeth Wilson has died after her house was damaged and so has the driver of the petrol tanker travelling through the village.'

Although we didn't know these people, it was still upsetting and our thoughts went out to their families. We later found out that Miss Robinson had also died and the lorry driver was Mr Lawrence Westwood from York. Nobody knew why the siren hadn't gone off and, of course, we couldn't have heard the plane over the noise of the mill. We found out that the pilot had circled the village before dropping one bomb, which struck Miss Robinson's house at the foot of the brow, and then the other fell in the roadway. And we heard how walls were cracked, roofing had been torn off and windows were shattered. About a dozen villagers received minor injuries as well.

'It's such a mess out there,' said Dad. 'The tanker's petrol caught alight and the post office suffered the blast too.'

'Is everyone all right?' asked Mum.

'The Postmaster was hit on the head and his daughters had a few cuts, but thankfully his wife was unhurt,' he told us.

All the injured were taken to the workhouse in Clitheroe, which is now Clitheroe Hospital, where they opened up an emergency centre.

The bombs had caused absolute destruction. And it wasn't just the outside of houses and buildings that had suffered but the inside too, as furniture had been flung about due to the force of the bomb. Gas and water mains had been broken, electric cables and telephone wires snapped; the chapel windows were also shattered.

The only saving grace was hearing no school children had been injured.

'Apparently, they all dived under their desks like they'd been told to do,' explained Dad. 'And they were lucky because just a day or two before they'd had the windows protected with wire netting.'

'Oh, thank the Lord!' gasped Mum.

That night, I went to bed and prayed for those who'd been killed and injured. I also thanked God that we'd been left unharmed. For a while, it didn't seem real what had happened. I mean, we always knew we were at war but this had made it real: *too* real.

Despite what had happened, I wandered down to the mill the next day, but I think it was a day or two before we all went back properly. The ceiling wasn't fixed but all the glass had been swept away. But it was heartbreaking, walking past the destroyed houses, and of course the bombing remained at the forefront of everyone's minds.

'I don't know how it got so low without anyone warning,' said one.

'My neighbour was just coming out of her front door to go to the bus stop when the explosion happened,' said another. 'She was lucky she only had a few cuts.'

No one knew if the pilot had flown over the mill, as it would have been too noisy to hear the plane, but the thought sent shivers down everyone's spines.

'Imagine if he'd dropped it on us,' said one. 'Doesn't bear thinking about!'

All week long, tales continued to be told about who'd seen the German Heinkel 111.

'He was so low you could see the swastika – and the pilot!' someone said.

'In fact, my neighbour said you could even see he was wearing goggles and a brown leather flying helmet,' added another.

Although scary for us, I think it must have been worse for those who actually saw the plane. At least us lot in the mill were oblivious – until the bomb dropped, of course – so we were spared the fear of knowing he was there and what might happen.

As you can imagine, the bombing remained on people's minds for a long time. It brought a lot of pain to our village so it was no surprise that speculation as to the bomber's motive was rife. Some thought that he was heading for Low Moor, since there was a barracks station there; others believed he was a lone bomber who became lost so had to offload before he flew back; and some said he was following the tanker that was driving through the village at the time. But to this day no one knows the real reason, and the pilot got away – I mean, it's not like there was anyone in Chatburn to shoot him down.

That day in the mill, our blackout curtains were put up and we had the lights on all the time. Although it was unlikely it would happen again, no one wanted to risk it. And in chapel, the Sunday following that dreaded day, we remembered those killed and injured by the bomb. It was a tough time for the villagers but we had no other choice but to carry on as best we could.

At first it was a little scary going back into the mill and working under the ceiling, but the blackout curtains helped. And with each day, it got easier. But a few months later, when the manager said we'd have to have another day off because of the shortage of work, the thought of losing money was just too much. Muriel and me were sick of it and so we went to the Labour Exchange – and we were in luck!

They needed volunteers for the munitions factories so we signed up. Now, I say 'volunteers', but that didn't mean like today when you did it for free as you got paid then. It just meant your employer had to let you work there as long as you were needed and then had to re-employ you afterwards.

'Sounds good to me!' I smiled.

I returned to the mill to tell the manager where I was going.

'Do you want to?' he asked.

'Yes,' I replied, trying not to sound too happy. In fact, I ended up working away for three years and there was nothing the mill could do about it.

The following week, I went to a training centre in Great Harwood for six weeks before being moved to Bristol Aircraft, which was situated in Carlton Mill, Clitheroe. Although Muriel and me had trained together, she had to go to a place in Clayton, which was a shame as we were hoping to work together. After that, we drifted apart but she remained living in Chatburn.

Arriving at the four-storey building, I was put 'on the line' on the ground floor, where my job was to build aeroplane engines. I was told the hours would be 7.30am to 7pm and we'd also have to do the night shift of 7.30pm to 7am. It sounded like hard work and a lot of responsibility but I wasn't put off and I couldn't wait to get started.

On my first day in February 1941, I wore trousers because it was winter and a navy overall with sleeves. I was put on a station with a young man my age called Alan, who was from Padiham. Each station had a man and a girl working together (this was necessary because the parts were so heavy you needed the strength of a man). We were given all the parts and we had to build up the engine from scratch and then it went off to the test house. But we weren't given training, just shown how to do it there and then.

'We'll be watching you build them and we will check them before you and us agree it's ready to be signed off,' explained an inspector. I couldn't believe what a big responsibility we'd been given so it was crucial we double-checked everything we did.

'It's like we're engineers!' I told Alan.

'Let's just hope it passes!' he laughed.

It was a fun job and I loved it. Not only was there a great sense of patriotic pride in doing something worthwhile, which we really had to think about and made a difference, but it was also nice working alongside men, as in the mill, apart from the odd tackler who came over, I'd worked solely with women. And it wasn't even about the ages in here as it was all mixed. It was just a good atmosphere and I got on with everyone but especially with two girls, Joan and Peggy. Joan was a little bit younger than Peggy and me but we all got on really well and spent most dinnertimes together.

'Shall we go to Howards for dinner?' Peggy would ask. 'I'll go and ask the others.'

Howards Dining Room was a café on Moor Lane, just two minutes away. We'd feast on steak pudding or meat pie followed by sponge pudding and custard or rice pudding.

We worked shifts, including nights, but I didn't mind. And we had to work six days a week so we either got a Saturday or Sunday off, but on Sunday my start time was too early to catch the bus so I had to walk.

'I'll come with you,' Dad offered one morning.

'OK, thanks,' I said.

It used to take me about 40 minutes and at first I didn't mind it, especially when it started to warm up and we had bright mornings, but soon the novelty wore off and so

Dad bought me a pushbike.

'There you go,' he smiled.

'Thanks!' I gasped.

But one thing about the factory was the spirit: all the people in there were so friendly and, if women weren't breaking into a good old sing-song, then we were having a laugh.

During one evening shift through the summer, we decided to nip out and take a walk. We always had a break from 12 to 1am and, if it was nice weather, we'd head outside. Well, on this particular night, there must have been about 10 or 12 of us and we were all linked up, walking back up the road to the factory when something soft shot between my legs and I screamed.

'What was *that?*' I screeched.

Now, because of the war there were no street lamps on, so if you can imagine the street was pitch black and we couldn't see a thing. And because it was so warm, I was wearing a skirt, and of course you couldn't get tights during the war so I was bare-legged.

As the group fell into a heap of giggles, one of them managed to say it was probably a black cat.

'You hope it was,' I cried, 'as no one can see what it was!'

And, although it frightened me half to death, we spent the remainder of the shift laughing about it.

But the night after when we returned to work we were in trouble.

'The people in the nearby cottages have complained about folk screaming in the night while they're trying to sleep,' our manager told us. 'They even went to the police!'

We tried to explain what had happened and, thankfully, the matter was dropped.

'Anyway, it was probably one of their flaming cats!' I cried.

Having so much fun at the munitions factory made me worry even more about the mill.

'I'm not going to want to go back,' I admitted to Mum.

The thought of having to work in that room with the same women as before made my heart sink. Now, I'm not knocking the ladies as they were nothing but kind and friendly to me for all the years I worked with them, and in truth were lovely women. It was just that I was a young girl and I wanted to be with people of my own age. I had nothing in common with them when they talked about their husbands and children.

Sometimes I'd ask Dad how his day at the mill had been.

'The same,' he'd reply. But other times he would tell me people had asked about me, especially Lizzie.

'That's nice,' I smiled. 'Tell her I said hello.'

There were some lovely people in there who I missed not seeing, but still my stomach knotted at the thought of being in there day in, day out in the same spot as before. It might sound daft but I wanted to stay working in the factory forever. Not only did I prefer the work, but I also got paid more for it, too. But I knew that wasn't possible, so, for the time being, I just got on with my job and tried not to think about the mill.

And any time the sirens went off we just carried on working. I remember feeling a little scared, especially after the mill incident, but I just got on with it. I don't think it happened that often.

Despite being at war and the obvious things like rationing and sirens, life went on as normally as it could. If I didn't see Muriel, then I'd go and meet my friend Ida, who lived in Clitheroe, and we'd go to the pictures at the Grand or the Palladium. It would cost one shilling, which would be five pence in today's money.

One particular Saturday night in January 1942, I'd gone to the pictures in Clitheroe with Ida. We were just coming out at about 10.30pm and I was heading back to the bus stop when the siren went off.

'What you going to do?' she asked.

'Well, wait for the bus,' I replied. 'It'll be here soon.'

To be honest, there was nothing much else

I could do besides go home with her but then I'd be stuck as this was the last bus of the night. The bus was due at quarter to the hour and I just prayed it would show up. I wasn't scared but, after the mill incident, I'd become a bit more wary. Still, I didn't think we were in any danger, as the last thing I thought was we'd be bombed again.

I think I must have told Ida to go home and, minutes later, three buses (like normal!) pulled up and everyone from the queue jumped on. And I can't remember if I felt frightened on the bus, or if anyone else was, but I suppose I knew it was the only way home. When it pulled up in the village, I must admit I'd never run home so fast!

It's odd thinking back because I suppose, even though the siren went off, life didn't suddenly stop as the bus was still being driven, although perhaps the driver knew we'd be stranded if he didn't. Most times you had a few minutes after the siren had gone off, and it was only a five-minute drive.

The next day, on 12 January 1942, as I headed into work, everyone was chatting.

'What's happened?' I asked Peggy.

'We were bombed last night,' she told me. 'They dropped four bombs down Henthorn, on Siddows, but thankfully no one was hurt.'

Suddenly, the war felt like it was getting

closer every day, and, even though the end meant returning to the mill, it couldn't come soon enough.

CHAPTER TWELVE

Friendships Forever

In February 1945, with a heavy heart I dragged my heels down Ribble Lane towards the mill. No longer needed in the munitions factory, I was on my way back. I could have gone home and cried when they told me I was no longer needed because I liked it so much. It had felt like an escape from my real working life and the last thing I wanted was to go back to that reality.

But I had to return to the mill, as I had no choice in the matter and you couldn't please yourself. Employers had a duty to take back those who had volunteered and we were expected to return. After all, I needed to work and the last thing I'd turn down was a job – even if I wasn't keen. As I've already explained, it wasn't like today, you just got on with it and were grateful you were earning. In theory, that was great as it meant no one was out of work, but for me it was a chore and I didn't want to go back. I'd had such fun in the factory that I wasn't keen to return to the mill and the people I worked with.

I headed straight to the office, where the manager – a short guy I didn't have much time for, but now struggle to remember his name – asked me, 'Do you want to come back?'

'No, I don't,' I replied honestly. 'And I'm only coming back if I get the top wage!'

Looking back, that was pretty brazen of me but I didn't care. I must have known they needed me more than I did them, or perhaps deep down I was hoping they'd say they *didn't* need me. But, when you reached the age of 25, you were put on the top wage, which meant I could go on piece work and make more money.

'OK,' he replied.

So, at least that was something good about coming back.

I assumed I'd be back on the same frames as before with the same women, so, when he led me to a different corner of the room, where a woman of about my age was standing at a frame (someone I knew from the village), I was pleasantly surprised.

'Hello,' she said.

Soon, three more women about my age and, again, familiar faces from the village turned up. Straight away it felt better than before. I don't know whether it was me being at ease because I was happier with where I'd been put or if the atmosphere in the mill had changed, but I assumed it must be the latter.

It was much better being with women around my age, especially when they broke into songs. They loved singing the old war songs, such as 'We'll Meet Again'. There was a lovely line in the song about smiling through, until the blue skies drive the dark clouds away, and it really resonated with me.

But the conditions hadn't changed and we were still hard done by, as it was a long day and hard work. This time around, it did feel that bit more manageable, though, so at least that was some consolation. And, while my working life was improving, the world was celebrating as the Second World War was declared over on 2 September 1945 with the surrender of Japan.

Once the street party celebrations had died down, a few months later, a new girl started at the mill and she was to become one of my closest friends.

Maureen Frankland was put opposite me to beam.

'Are you OK to show her the ropes, Marjorie?' the manager asked.

'Yes, of course,' I replied.

'Thanks,' Maureen smiled. 'I'm hoping I'll pick it up quick!'

Maureen was 14 and lived in the village, and we instantly got on. While I showed her what to do, we chatted about our family and friends and realised we knew the same people. She was a joy to work across from (and train) and soon came out of herself when the tapers (the man who did the job after a beamer who puts the pattern in) coming over tried to tease her.

'Just give it to them back!' I smiled.

Although Maureen was younger than me, we always got on and there was always an amusing tale to be told about her. I remember one New Year's Day when she never showed up.

'That's odd,' I said to the others. Now, I know I've already told you how some people looked a bit worse for wear on this day, but this wasn't like Maureen. I mean, she'd have been no older than 15, so it wasn't as if she would have been out, and she always turned up for work.

At lunchtime, there was still no sign so I went to ask Maureen's dad Billy, but I couldn't find him either.

'Never came in,' said one of the workers.

'Oh, right,' I said.

The next day, in sloped a sheepish-looking Maureen.

'I slept in!' she laughed. 'We all did and even my dad didn't come in.'

'I did wonder where you were,' I said.

'Oh, we're in right bother,' she added. 'We've just been to explain but he [the manager] doesn't believe us – he thinks we just wanted the day off!'

Another time, one Wednesday in February 1947, we were having one of the coldest Februaries recorded, with heavy snowfall. Lots of villages became cut off and isolated so, when Maureen never came back after dinner that day, I was worried. She'd been there all morning so it wasn't like she was poorly, as I'd have known. So, when one of the tapers came up, I was telling him about it. 'I can't understand it,' I said. 'Why would she not come back?' Unbeknown to me, this guy went back to the tape room, where Maureen's dad Billy worked, and said, 'Marjorie is worried as your Maureen hasn't come back. Is she not well?' Well, Billy didn't know anything about this!

As the hours went by, more and more people were getting worried about Maureen. 'What if she's got stuck or fallen in the snow?' I fretted. But, with Chatburn being the small village it is, and most people knowing each other, word soon spread back to the factory that Maureen was safe – and in the pictures with her friend Nellie!

'What's she like?' I laughed, shaking my head, but relieved she was safe. And the next day, when she turned up again, I heard the full tale.

'We'd gone home for dinner and, because Mum was off work with her bad leg and Dad worked in a different room, I thought we'd get away with bunking off,' she explained.

'So, me and Nellie told Mum we were heading back to work sooner – we left just after 1pm – so we could throw snowballs before work, but instead we caught the bus to Clitheroe and went to the pictures.'

'Everyone was worried about you,' I said.

'I *know!*' she replied. 'There was us sitting nice and warm in the pictures when suddenly one of the women who worked there came over and said, "Are you Maureen Frankland and Nellie Smith?" So we said we were and she said we were wanted on the phone. I had to follow her to the office and Dad was on the phone. "Oh, you're there, are you? Well, come home at once!" he shouted. I'd never heard Dad snap at me like that before.

'So, feeling worried, I put the phone down and went back and told Nellie we had to go, to which she replied, "Well, this is almost finished so we may as well watch the end of it as we're in trouble whatever!" I knew she had a point so we stayed a bit longer but when we came out there were no buses because the snow was as high as the wall. We couldn't walk on the pathway and had to walk in the middle of the road so I made her walk all the way home with me, even though she lived in Clitheroe. I told her I wasn't facing my mum and dad on my own! And when we finally got home, my mum just said, "Wait till your dad comes home!" So the pair of us were sat waiting, and I was frightened to death and crying, but when he walked in all he did was laugh!'

It had caused a bit of a commotion in Chatburn as word spread that the girls were missing so, when the driver of the bus they'd caught came back to Chatburn and heard, word got back to Billy.

'I'm so daft I never gave it a second thought,' Maureen giggled.

Being young and naïve, she thought her dad would never find out. I don't think she got into any trouble with the mill manager, though. In fairness, she had suffered enough as she never lived it down. From then on, each Wednesday, one of the tapers would come over before dinnertime and ask, 'Are you OK today, Maureen? Will you be coming back?' But they were only teasing and it's nothing she wouldn't have expected; everybody would laugh about it. And, compared to today's standards, it was nothing, really – I think it was the only bad thing Maureen ever did!

When Maureen started at the mill, it felt as though times were already changing as she started on 24 shillings, unlike my 8. And, because she was 14 when she began work, she didn't need to work Saturday morning and, by 1948, when she reached the age of 16, the Saturday working hours had been abolished.

Although it was great having two full days away from the mill, at first it was weird not having to work. Having a longer weekend was good, but it did mean that dreaded Sunday feeling about returning to the mill got worse. But at least I had Maureen. It was great working with her and the more we got to know each other, the more we seemed to share a common ground in that we both believed we shouldn't have been in the mill – even though, stupidly, we'd chosen it for ourselves! However, unlike me, Maureen hadn't needed to come into the mill. She admitted she could have done hairdressing but she knew she would have to work all day Saturday and she didn't want to do that because she wanted to go out with her friends.

Like me, Maureen had been to Ribblesdale Senior School, and in the few years since I'd been there attitudes had changed slightly, so she had more options than me. Time had moved on and nobody had forced her into the mill; instead, she had come of her own free will. Years later she admitted to me it was probably a foolish thing to do, but she was young and impressionable and, as most of the villagers, including her friends, worked in there, she just thought she would too.

'I was quite happy not to work Saturday, but, once I got in here and realised what it was like, I wished I hadn't been so silly,' she told me later.

Nevertheless, she and I had some really good times and, like I said, we thought the same way. It wasn't that we thought highly of ourselves but we always believed we shouldn't have gone in the mill, as we weren't cut out for it.

'I think we're more cut out for the finer things in life,' I teased.

Each day was the same: we'd have a gossip, some banter with the male workers and a bit of a laugh. There was one guy, who worked near to Maureen and me and he was such a laugh. We'd have banter with him all the time and it just made the day go quicker. It's why everyone did it!

'Aye oop, what about them two carrying on in t'shed?' he'd say, winking.

'Give up!' I'd laugh.

People were always gossiping and joking about people carrying on together but I never saw anything – I'm sure all sorts went on, though!

Slowly, but steadily, things started to improve in the mill. I can't remember what year it was, but our Wakes Week holiday was made up into two weeks instead of the week it had been, and the working hours changed to 8am until 12.30pm and then 1.30pm until 5pm.

'About time,' I said. 'We work hard enough, we deserve it!'

Even though the bosses never threw us a

Christmas party, as the years went by, we used to organise our own little bash and would put paper trimmings around our frames. But I don't ever remember a mill party, and any days out we had during Wakes Week was always organised by ourselves.

Chitchat in the mill either revolved around your husband, children, what was on the wireless or what you'd done at the weekend. Getting a television of your own was a big deal, though. Having a TV set was something most of the workers couldn't afford.

'We've got our own,' Maureen beamed one Monday morning. 'Jack's parents have rented us a TV.' (Maureen had got married in 1954 and was living with Jack's parents until they got a house of their own – they eventually moved back to Chatburn.)

'That's nice of 'em,' I replied.

'I *know!*' she gasped.

'It's al'reet for some!' one of the women smirked.

'Well, Maureen, that'll be you not going to the picture house for a while then!' joked one of the women.

'Aye, you're right there!' she laughed.

Before I knew it, the years had whizzed by, and during my time in the mill I'd seen King George V's Silver Jubilee, the invention of television, the introduction of the NHS and

Queen Elizabeth II's Coronation – all of which had been hot topics among the workers. But over the years one thing close to my heart was watching my friends from the mill getting married and some of them becoming parents. Now, back then, we didn't shower them with gifts or big nights out, but we always tried to have a whip round and at least give them something, however small.

And, although I had a few romances along the way, no man had ever been quite enough to steal my heart. So, one afternoon when Jack Wilkinson came over to Gladys and me and asked if we wanted to pick some strawberries from his garden, I never thought anything of it.

Gladys was about a year older than me and married. I can't remember now how long we'd been working together but she was nice and we got on. By then, Maureen had left the mill to have her daughter Karen, although she came back later. So, it was nice that I got on so well with Gladys. Both of us knew this Jack fella as he worked as a labourer, close to our frames. He'd not been in the mill so long but he always passed the time of day with me and seemed pleasant enough.

Jack wasn't over tall, but he had a nice smile and brown hair. Nice natured, he wasn't loud, as some men could be. He was a trained butcher but he'd been called up and on his return came into the mill.

'Aye, do you fancy it, Marjorie?' asked Gladys.

'Ooh yes, that'd be lovely! Ta,' I said.

So, once we'd had tea, Gladys and I walked down to Jack's house and he led us out to his garden to pick some strawberries. I had a nice evening but, as far as I was concerned, we were just friends. So, the next day when he asked us again, we agreed, but just as I was finishing my tea Gladys came across to knock for me.

'I can't go to Jack's,' she said. Gladys's husband wanted to go to the pictures, so, of course, she had to do that because in those days you tended to do what your husband wanted. 'I feel awful, though, as I said we'd go.'

'Not to worry,' I replied. 'I'll just go.'

But Jack didn't seem bothered that I'd come to visit on my own and it was nice being able to talk. I found out he had been born at the local Brown Cow pub, and his mother had been an invalid since he was 12 years old. After his father died and Jack's twin brother married and moved to Ireland, he had looked after his mother. She was in a wheelchair and he had to do everything for her before she had passed away a few years ago. Even though I only looked upon Jack as a friend, I soon learned what a decent, kind fella he was, so, when he asked me out, I decided to say yes. It was 1955, and I was 35 years old and Jack was 38.

I knew Jack was a keeper, and my parents liked him, so I was over the moon when we decided to get married. But I don't remember him proposing, it was more something we agreed on because we got married sooner than we should have done. Jack was living on his own and I was still at home when a house on Ribblesdale View came up for rent. One of the mill houses, it was a lot cheaper to rent than a council house, but I'm afraid far too many years have passed for me to remember how much it was.

'Let's go and look at it,' I suggested to Jack.

I remember walking up the few stone steps to the front door with butterflies in my stomach – I was so excited! When we opened the front door, it was dirty and there were cobwebs everywhere.

'Oh, *no!*' I sighed, disappointed. 'It's filthy.'

'It's fine,' soothed Jack, 'that's easily cleaned.'

And he was right: the owners of the mill had the house repaired and installed a bath before we moved in.

So, once we had found the house, it was time to get married. Back then, there wasn't all the same fuss as today and we were just happy to have a quiet wedding in the Methodist church. The night before was like any normal Friday night. In those days, there was no such thing as a hen do; I'm not even sure the girls did anything for me at work (you didn't then). Instead, I just went home, like normal, and spent the night in with my parents – and most probably had a bath!

The next day, on 3 April 1957, Dad walked me down the aisle towards my future husband. My dress was blue lace with a matching hat and lined with forget-me-knots around the front. At £8 I thought I'd paid the earth for it! My friend Ida was my bridesmaid but, as I've said, it wasn't a big affair like they have today.

Once we were married, Jack never expected me to do everything around the house: 'We're both working so we'll share the duties,' he said. For that time, he was very forward thinking and a great husband. He was also a great cook, much better than me! I think, because he'd looked after his mother for so long, he was used to doing chores, especially the cooking. For him, it was second nature and not necessarily just the woman's job.

'I don't know what you got me for!' I used to say, teasing, as he stood beside me in the kitchen, chopping veg.

'To look after you,' he'd smile.

I felt so lucky, and even more so when a few years later the offer to buy our home came up. The previous mill owners wanted to sell off the houses when they sold the mill to Smith & Nephew so they were giving all their tenants first refusal.

'We have to do it,' I told Jack. And we did, buying it for £1,200 – a figure that seems unimaginable today.

Meanwhile, I ploughed along in the mill and over time I saw lots of people come and go, and I'd worked with lots of characters. But the one person I missed was Maureen, so, when she came back to work after having her daughter, I was over the moon.

'Back where you belong!' I teased.

'Oh, *great!*' she sighed. 'I didn't want to come back but the manager came and asked me and even said I could start a bit later.'

'Well, I'm pleased you're back,' I smiled. 'It wasn't the same without you.'

And that's the effect the mill had: you didn't really want to be in there but it always pulled you back in. I was just grateful I had my Jack and Maureen in there with me. And, whatever I thought about the mill, it was something I'd never have swapped and, to this day, I still count my blessings.

In 1980, when I was 60 years old, I finished at the mill. I was presented with a bracelet and bunch of flowers for my 46 years of service. It wasn't tough saying goodbye to the place but it was to the people inside it, especially Maureen as we'd worked together for over 50 years. But she is to this day still a very dear friend, someone I see often. Sadly, I lost Jack in 1968 after just 11 wonderful years of marriage and we never had children as it was something that never happened.

Reflecting back over my life now, I do wonder whether I would have been better off doing a job like sewing. But then again, if I'd done that, I wouldn't have had the life I did, or, more importantly, met the same people. Although I was glad to leave the mill when I did, I'm grateful for what it gave me: friendship, a loving husband, a home (I still live in the same house Jack and I bought) and a regular income. The conditions may have been long and gruelling but the banter and workers got you through and that's something some jobs don't have today. Also, it wasn't all bad as there was some goodwill from employers to employees when it came to rent and I also have a pension, courtesy of Smith & Nephew, who took over the mill before I retired.

The closure of the mill in 1991 was sad but no surprise. I think it was inevitable – there'd been trouble brewing since I was there, with cutting jobs and not replacing workers. For a couple of years, there were rumours it was going to close. And, because Chatburn was one of the last mills to close, the pending closure was even reported on *Newsnight* as they'd visited the mill to speak to workers, including Maureen. I just felt bad for the workers who relied on the wage and those who had worked there all their lives and left without a penny, such as Maureen, who at 59 was still earning. Over the last few years, the mill had been replacing workers, especially weavers, with quicker and more modern machinery, and all the while the threat of closure was looming.

If I'd had children, I wouldn't have wanted them to work in the mill but at that time we knew no different and so we accepted it – something I doubt would happen today.

I dragged my heels all the way to the mill. 'I can't do it!' I sulked. She sighed and shook her head. My heart sank. Of course, I'd seen the mill hundreds of times before, but now it was different – now I was going in. I'd never seen a place so depressing; I wanted to cry.

Part Four:

Maureen Wilson

CHAPTER THIRTEEN

Growing Up

My name is Maureen Wilson, but I was born into this world as Maureen Brennan on 17 November 1936 and that makes me the grand old age of 77. I've seen a lot in those years, and experienced so many different things. For one, I'm a mother to three boys, Steven, Stewart and Andrew, and have nine wonderful grandchildren. They are the most important people in my life. I've decided to share my story about the mills because it was one of the happiest times of my life but, most importantly, it shaped my future. I first met my husband during this time, and now I want to share my story with my family, as a reminder of their history. So, let me take you back to the start of my journey in Blackburn.

For those not sure of the geography, the Lancashire town is 9 miles from Preston and 20 miles from Greater Manchester. Before the Industrial Revolution, Blackburn was a mere village but, between 1750 and 1850, the population increased as it became one of the great cotton weaving centres of the world. The Blackburn I was born into was a typical industrial town, with numerous tall chimneys depositing smoke and smog over the entire place, and row upon row of terraced houses squashed together. Through the centre of the town flowed a polluted river and against this backdrop were the railway line and viaduct, with constant noise and the smoke of the steam trains adding to the polluted atmosphere. The town was also split by the Leeds and Liverpool Canal passing through the centre and benefited from a good transport system, including an improved bus service as well as the railway. At this time, the other predominant industries were coal mining, brick making, brewing and chemicals, but there was also mass unemployment in the town. Lancashire was once booming, but now there was a decline in the demand for cotton and that meant some of the mills were closing down.

But it wasn't all doom and gloom. The town's council had instigated the construction of new council houses to replace the traditional back-to-back slum houses built to accommodate the mill workers, and new industries were appearing in the shape of engineering (Mullards), paint making (Walpamur) and a new Royal Ordnance Factory, which would develop considerably as the Second World War approached. Sport was very popular, especially the local football team, Blackburn Rovers, who played in the

Football League Division 1 and were quite famous.

I was born in a simple two up, two down in the suburb of Wensley Falls, to my mother Elizabeth and father Joseph Brennan, who went by the name of Joe. Dad was tall and dark, with slicked-back hair but he'd suffered from TB (back then, they called it 'consumption'). I'm not sure when he got it, but it was before my brother Terry and me were born, so he always looked gaunt and ill to me and had a permanent cough. Mum, on the other hand, was slim with auburn hair and a bit of a looker.

The pair, Blackburn born and bred, had known each other as kids because they used to hang out on Corporation Park – a popular place where children played, including myself later in life. Joe was three years older than Mum, and when she was 18 they got married. Soon after, in July 1934, their first-born, Terry, came along. With his mousey-coloured hair, he looked just like any other little boy – a bit nondescript, I suppose, if I'm honest. A couple of years later, when Mum was 20, she had me.

Obviously, I don't remember anything of my infant years but I do know our Sylvia, my sister, was born on 30 September 1938. I was only two years old at the time so my memory of her birth and Mum being pregnant is hazy, to say the least. Mum told me when I turned three we moved to another two up, two down on St Paul's Street. It was a better area and the house, although the same size as the previous one, was a bit nicer.

Anyway, two months before my third birthday, on 1 September 1939, something much greater happened than any milestone in my life: the Second World War broke out. But, while we fought against the Nazis, I was of course oblivious to it. I just carried on like any toddler would, clinging to my mummy's arm and eating what was put in front of me. Oh, and starting at St Paul's Primary School, which was just across the road from our house. I wish I could tell you more about my days at school, but, sadly, I can't. A bit like the war details, I'm afraid, long since disappeared. The memory may have come back to me when I was younger, but now it's definitely not there! I do remember my first day, though. I was crying but when I got inside my tears dried up when I saw a big, roaring fire; suddenly I was all warm and cosy.

In fact, it wasn't until I got to about the age of six that things become a little clearer and I can remember stuff, like hearing the sounds of the sirens.

'What's that, Mummy?' I asked.

'Come on, let's go!' she cried.

Before I knew it, Mum had swept Sylvia into her arms and then shoved her in the pram. Telling Terry to grab me, we dashed outside and across our street.

'It's an air raid shelter,' Terry said, as we – and most of our neighbours – scrambled to get inside to safety.

But Mum didn't like our street communal shelter. It had a thick brick wall and a reinforced concrete roof. Cold, damp and smelly, I don't remember us going in it that often. I do have recollections of the frightening sound when a bomb dropped, though. But, from what I've been told in later life, thankfully, it wasn't that often.

Somewhere along the line, I remember Mum taking us on a steam train to Barrow-in-Furness, in Cumbria. To this day, I don't know how she paid for the train and it was the first time I'd ever been on one. As our Terry, our Sylvia and me sat in the carriage Mum just kept telling us to come away from the door. I think the window must have been down (that's what they did in those days, not like today) and she didn't want the steam from the train blowing on us and making us dirty. I'm not sure why we went but I do know Dad didn't come with us. He wasn't in the war either because of his TB. We stayed with a friend of Mum's and we must have been there a while as I remember the others and me went to a nursery school.

Soon enough, though, we were back home

and times were tough – tough for everyone, mind you – but they were even tougher for our family.

Rationing may have affected the UK, but the war played no part in our lack of food. For example, I thought eating black treacle butties or sugar butties was normal. At school, we got free dinners, and my teacher told me and some of the other children to bring in a bowl. It was great because they filled it with food, which I was allowed to eat once I got home.

Now and again, Mum would send me to the top shop (our local corner shop) to get a loaf of bread or a pork pie. And, on the rare occasion when we had a fish supper from the chippie, we always shared it.

Our clothes were tatty and we'd wear them until they fell apart. Mum bought them from a second-hand stall on Blackburn market. She paid about one shilling for a dress or a pair of socks, which would be about five pence in today's money. Most of the kids I knew were in the same position as us, so it wasn't something I ever thought about. To me, it was just the norm.

I wasn't sure what Dad did to earn money, and Mum wasn't working because she was too busy looking after Terry, Sylvia and me. Our house was always freezing and we didn't have heating. We just had the coal fire in the front room and in the kitchen there was a gas cooker. Of course, we didn't have a bathroom either (people didn't, in those days). Instead, all our washing was done at the sink downstairs with cold water and a bath. I say 'bath', but it was actually a large tin container, I suppose, which we put in front of the fire once a week.

One thing I did know, despite my young age, was that Mum and Dad weren't a good couple. Some nights, usually after Dad had come home from the pub, I'd be shivering in bed, under the flimsy blanket and our coats piled on top of us, and I could hear them rowing downstairs. But Dad was never mean to me, and I liked him.

It was no surprise, though, when, one day in the winter of 1943, when I was seven, Mum told us we were moving to Grandma's house. Although there was no mention of Dad coming, I didn't feel upset because I was too young to really understand. I even had to change schools and went to St Michael's, but I was too young to really understand or be sad about leaving my friends because I soon made new ones. Anyway, I enjoyed school and I remember St Michael's had a sloping playground, which was always fun to play on!

The day we left, Mum told me to put my clothes in a bag. Not that I had much, or anything else for that matter. And I don't know what happened to the bit of furniture we had. I'm not sure whether I was too young to understand, or the thought of where we were heading was too exciting to feel upset, but I'm afraid I didn't feel sad about leaving home or my dad. You see Grandma lived in an area of Blackburn called Whalley Range, just 10 minutes' walk from our house.

Oh, and her house was huge! It was like a palace compared to our dingy home. But best of all, she had a bathroom. Pure luxury!

'This is brilliant!' I beamed, as I raced up the front steps to Grandma's front door.

Now, my poor grandma must have felt like tearing her hair out when our tribe turned up. You see, Grandma – her real name was Rose Hough – had gone on to have seven more children after my mum. Grandma was kind and loving. A plump lady, she always wore a pinny around her waist, with two pockets on the front. She had my uncle Fred, uncle Tommy and uncle Harold – who, when we arrived, like most young men were fighting for our country – and my aunty Rose, aunty Marie, uncle Walter and aunty Dot (Walt and Dot were only a few years older than me) were still at home. And not forgetting my dear granddad Jo, Grandma's brother Arthur, who was blind, and her brother-in-law, Uncle Herbert, who looked *really* old to me but I bet they were only in their 60s. I thought my uncle Walt was the best thing since sliced bread; he was lovely.

Fair and stocky, with a dimple in his chin, he was nice-looking and such a great dancer. In fact, I think I had a crush on him. Aunt Dot was plump (bless her, she lost all her teeth at 16 because she ate too many sweets) but Aunt Marie was my favourite. I'd sit on her bed and watch her getting glammed up to go out dancing. I loved her to the day she died, aged 86, in May 2013.

I can't remember how long we were there or where we all slept, but I cherished every single minute. Granddad had an allotment so we ate better than we did at home. My mouth watered at the smell of vegetables boiling on the stove and, when he caught a rabbit, well, it was like Christmas!

Sadly, though, I know we couldn't have been there long enough (to my child's mind, I might add) as my poor grandma had enough family to be looking after, so she probably didn't want us under her feet too. Before I knew it, we were moving to another house. This time it was on Fisher Street in Blackburn and 20 minutes away from Grandma's house by foot (we had to walk there because we couldn't afford the bus). Mum was renting the new place from a landlord at £1 and 25 shillings a week. I was grateful to have a roof over my head, but it was awful.

Everyone on Fisher Street was poor. Our

house was the end one in a row of terraces. These houses lined the streets of Blackburn, having been built for workers in the mills. So, it was no surprise that next door to our house was one such mill: Fisher Street Mill. That was nothing unusual for our town; I'm not sure how many mills there were in Blackburn at that time but you always lived within spitting distance of one. But it was a horrible, big building that looked depressing and murky. And, when I watched the workers leaving at night, they seemed dirty and downtrodden.

I suppose this was my first taste of a mill. And, even at the age of eight, it didn't look an appealing place to work.

Anyhow, our house was cold and sparse; we had no carpets or lino, just hard wooden floors. I don't know where the little bit of furniture we had came from but it was old and tatty. We had a square wooden table with knobbly legs that stood in the living room – no sideboard or anything – with two chairs. Our bedrooms consisted of just a bed; I didn't even have a wardrobe to hang my clothes in.

For some reason, in the living room there was a radiogram, a piece of furniture that combined a valve radio and a record player (we didn't have one of those in our last place). We had some old records and would listen to Paul Temple, the fictional character on the BBC radio serial.

We soon got settled there, living without Dad, but one morning I came down to breakfast and he was there.

'Hello, love,' he smiled.

As I spooned porridge into my mouth, I just smiled back. I wouldn't have dreamt of questioning him or Mum. Anyhow, I didn't care; it was just nice having him back home.

And, in 1944, Mum gave birth to another little girl, Pat. I didn't really think much of having another baby in the house but I had no choice!

They were good parents and I loved them both dearly but they were always rowing and falling out. And I remember one time Dad kicked a black puppy down the stairs. I don't know how we came to have it, but as the helpless little creature toppled its way down the wooden stairs I was horrified.

The truth was it was the drink, although he wasn't violent and never raised his fists to my siblings or me. It was Mum who ruled the roost and dished out the smacks. If one of us was naughty, or gave her back-chat, she'd give us a good hiding but that didn't stop me from misbehaving, though. And Sylvia and me would argue every night over whose turn it was to wash up. 'You little sod!' Mum'd shout, clouting us round the head. Dad was soft with us kids, but he wasn't a good drunk. And, while he was out drinking, Mum was no angel.

Mum started gallivanting at the dance halls. A popular place to go, it was where the American soldiers stationed here hung out, wooing the local ladies with their fancy dance moves and charm. But it was what everyone did then. So, it was no surprise when Dad left again; they just didn't seem good for each other. But, without his wage, Mum struggled.

At one point, I remember she sold our sweet rations so she could buy basic food. I wasn't upset as we'd never had sweets, and my belly was so empty I was just glad of food. She had no other choice but to get a job and, with four kids to raise, her only option was bar work because she could do that at night. Before starting a family, Mum had worked in the mill as a spinner but she couldn't do that now.

So, once we'd had our tea, it became a regular routine whereby Mum would march us around to Grandma's (that bit I didn't mind, I should add), but it was the walking home at night that I hated. She'd collect us at 11pm and, as she pushed Pat in the pram, we'd walk either side of her.

Just at the top of our street was an American Army base. In the day, it was bustling with army men and, even at night, it was common to pass them in the street. They looked so smart in their uniforms. With their money and style, most people, especially us kids, were in awe of them.

'Have you got any gum, chum?' Terry and me would shout. It was strips of chewing gum. Although we were only seven or eight, we knew the soldiers had brought loads of the stuff over from the States; they were so friendly and generous. Terry and I were over the moon when they threw us a packet.

'Thanks, Mister!' we cried.

Other nights walking home I'd be cold and tired, so Mum would make us sing to help keep us awake.

'Come on, let's sing "Pedro the Fisherman",' she'd say and then she'd start singing.

I did love the upbeat song but, as I dragged my heels with tiredness, singing was the last thing I wanted to be doing.

Cold and hungry, by the time we reached home my tiny bones were chattering.

The trouble was, I knew there'd be no respite because, when we got home, our house would be freezing. Ooh, it was cold! I dashed straight up those wooden stairs, stripped off my clothes so fast and jumped into a freezing-cold bed. I didn't bother brushing my teeth or wiping my face with cold water.

But the flimsy sheet, or it was more likely we just had our coats on the bed, was no match for the harsh northern temperature. And we didn't have thick pyjamas, like now. Oh, no! At best, I'd keep my knickers on.

I slept in the bed with our Sylvia, Terry was in a camp bed in the same room and our Pat was in the front bedroom with Mum. My feet were like ice. And, even with the body heat of our Sylvia, I don't think our bones had warmed by the time we nodded off. But you just got used to sleeping with a chill. After all, we had no other choice: being cold and hungry was the norm.

In the morning, we got ourselves out of bed and came downstairs for porridge with salt, and on odd days – if we were lucky – we'd have toast if there was any bread left, and a cup of tea. We were lucky having the baby as it meant Mum got concentrated orange juice from the clinic and more milk: national dried milk, like powder. Nonetheless, we couldn't be fussy.

We children walked to school together and walked back by ourselves at the end of the day. Mum never came to meet us – that was unheard of in those days. Back home, we played snakes and ladders, or if the weather was fine then we skipped rope outside. Despite not having much, I always remember being happy but it was a daily battle.

I remember on a few occasions Mum would suddenly shout, 'Hide! And keep quiet!' As the four of us fled, there would be a knock at the door. Mum would just smile and put her finger to her lips, so the young ones knew to keep quiet as we all ducked down under the kitchen table.

'Who's that, Mummy?' asked Pat.

'It's the cheque lady,' Mum replied.

The cheque lady used to come round and drop off cheques. It was money on tick. Trouble was, Mum didn't have the money to pay her back. She wasn't dishonest and, once she had the money, she always repaid her. It was just on some visits she couldn't.

Even at my tender age I could see that Mum was ashamed of having to hide. She'd have paid it if she'd got it but, instead, she'd rather feed us. One day, she became so desperate that she took hold of our Sylvia and me and marched us outside.

'We're going to see your dad!' she fumed.

At the time, Dad was seeing a woman called Mary, who lived just around the corner, but I couldn't tell you what she looked like for I never met her. When we arrived, the door was open. In those days, everybody knew their neighbours and there was a sense of trust so it was common for people not to lock their door and this door was open, too. As we stepped inside there was no sign of Dad or his female friend. But there, on the side, was the rent book.

Before I knew it, Mum had reached over

and grabbed it.

'Come *on!*' she ordered, as she shooed us quickly out the door.

To this day, I don't know how much – or if any – money was in there but I know Mum didn't care. At the most there may have been about £1 and 25 shillings, and that would have meant she could have bought us bread, potatoes and even beans. After all, we were desperate. It wasn't the honest thing to do, but Mum was raising us kids by herself, as Dad didn't give Mum any money for us when he wasn't living at home. I reckon she thought it was payback for Dad walking out on us.

But, on 8 May 1945, a glimmer of hope spread across the air when the Second World War in Europe was over. I was nine years old. Although the country rejoiced in celebration, the war hadn't really affected me as I'd never known anything different. If anything, us kids (the poor ones, anyway) liked it because it was the only time we had things like chewing gum, thanks to the Yank soldiers.

'So, Hitler has been stopped?' I asked Mum.

'Yes,' she told me. 'And we're having a street party to celebrate!'

While the country went crazy, neighbours rallied round to buy bunting and food and drink, such as jelly, custard, sausage rolls and orange cordial. Our street party was brilliant. In fact, it featured in the local paper, the *Lancashire Evening Telegraph*, for being the best one. Someone even lit a bonfire and made a Hitler for the guy on top! Anyhow, although the whole country was celebrating winning the war, we still had our own daily battle: survival.

The end of the war didn't stop rationing just like that. And, for us, it didn't end our poverty. So, it helped when one night there was a knock at the door. Mum opened it and a man was standing there.

'How many children have you got, Missus?' he asked. 'And what size feet do they have?'

Mum replied, and seconds later the man passed her four pairs of black patent and leather lace-up shoes.

'There you go,' he said.

They were shoes that had been repaired by foreign prisoners of war.

'Thank you,' Mum smiled.

And, even though they were second-hand, us kids didn't care.

'For *us?*' I cried, as Mum passed me a pair.

I couldn't remember the last time I'd seen a pair of shoes so shiny. But we were still desperately poor so Mum had to keep working at the pub.

Somewhere along the line, Dad must have

reappeared because in January 1946 our Pauline was born, but even a new baby couldn't stop the rows. Not surprisingly, he didn't stick around. And without Dad's wage Mum struggled again.

But, by the time I reached 11, we no longer had to make the nightly trek to Grandma's house. Instead, Mum left Terry and me at home to watch the others. But I didn't mind: to be honest, I didn't question it. Mum needed to work, and I would much rather stay indoors all night than be dragged home later in the cold.

By now, I was at Bangor Street School, the secondary modern. I don't know whether I was looking forward to it or not, but I know Mum had to get my uniform from the cheque lady and I soon made lots of friends. The following year, as I approached my twelfth birthday, for me it was just like any other day. I didn't get anything for my birthday; I never had – we were too poor. There was never a card or a cake. At most, Mum would simply wish me 'Happy Birthday'. But I wasn't bothered; Mum just didn't have the money and I understood that. After all, how can you miss something you've never had in the first place? I knew some friends from school got cake or a present for their special day, but I was never jealous as I knew, for us, it was the norm not to.

That Christmas, Mum took us all to

Ragged School, on Bent Street. I don't remember any of my friends from school going, but it was fine. This was a school for under-privileged kids and we got an apple, orange and chocolate coins.

'Thank you!' I squealed, made up that I was getting so much.

And the day just got better for we arrived home to find our uncle Harold waiting for us.

'Here you go,' he smiled, handing us a present. 'Happy Christmas!'

'Wow!' I gushed, as I tore open the wrapping paper to find a sewing set and a Ludo board game.

Mum did her best but as I've said before we had nothing so that Christmas was one of the best.

The following January, I came in from school one day with Terry and Sylvia to find Mum crying.

'Oh, Mum, what's the matter?' I asked, concerned.

'Come here,' she said, pulling us all towards her. 'I've got something to tell you.'

My heart sank – I thought she was poorly. But before I could speak she said, 'Someone's coming for you and you're going away for a while – but not for long. You're going somewhere nice and you'll be looked after, but I won't be there.'

I couldn't believe what she was saying; I didn't want to go anywhere else.

'What you doing? Where you going?' I cried. By now, all of us were blubbing like babies.

Next thing, there was a knock at the door and in walked a well-dressed woman we'd never seen before. Mum explained she was a social worker and she'd come to take us into care. One of the neighbours must have reported her for leaving us kids by ourselves while she went out to work; I couldn't believe it.

'We're ready,' the woman told Mum.

As she picked up Pauline and walked outside, Mum stood up.

'Ta-ra,' she said, trying to be strong. I think if she'd have hugged us she might have broken down.

Shuffling outside, we found a vehicle resembling a sit-up ambulance. We didn't take anything with us, just went as we were, still dressed in our school uniform which for me and our Sylvia consisted of a gym slip, white blouse, navy mac, grey knee socks and black lace-up shoes. Us five kids were sobbing as we piled into this vehicle and off it sped. I don't think any of us spoke, we were too busy crying and too frightened about what was going to happen.

We drove towards Queen's Park Hospital. Just by the hospital were three cottage homes. The social worker told us that one was for boys, the other for girls and one for the toddlers. The worst thing was that, because our Pauline was only a baby, she had to go to Queen's Park Hospital. That was heartbreaking as we didn't see her again for nine months.

Terry was taken to the boys' cottage, our Pat to the toddlers' one and Sylvia and me to the girls'. As we were shooed inside, I stepped onto the shiniest brown lino I'd ever seen – I could see my face in it. At the same time an amazing smell hit me.

'What is that?' I whispered. Ooh, it was wonderful!

'Polish,' replied a woman, smiling. 'It's when we've dusted and cleaned the furniture.'

I'd never been in a room – or building – so clean. Cosy, with lots of furniture inside, it looked like the home of my dreams. The house had six or eight bedrooms, and I think there were twelve girls there in total.

A woman stepped forward and introduced herself as 'Mother'. A biggish woman with a matronly look, in my young eyes I'd have put an age of 60 on her but she was probably only in her 40s! Warm and friendly, she explained in a soft voice what was going to happen next.

'Right, first things first, we are going to take you upstairs and give you a bath. Then we'll get you a nightie to wear – or if you prefer pyjamas, that's fine,' she said. 'Then you'll have a little bit of supper before we get you to your bed and, in the morning, we'll sort out some clothes for you.'

I couldn't believe what I was hearing. My tears had dried up and now a big smile was painted across my face: my own bed, a bath, pyjamas … it was as if I was on a luxury holiday. I almost burst with joy! And as I basked in my own bath, in hot soapy water that smelled clean and fresh, not like the smelly soap we had, my sadness faded away. This was heaven! In our house we washed in the sink, or as we called it, the 'slop stone'.

And as I curled up in bed, by myself, in a fresh clean nightdress I had the best night's sleep of my life. To this day, that was the only time I had a bed to myself.

The next morning, we were kitted out with new clothes and I was given a new uniform for school. Just because I was in care didn't mean that we didn't carry on as normal. For the first time ever, my belly was full and I smelled clean and fresh; I was never cold and we got pocket money, too. It was only sixpence a week (two-and-a-half pence in today's money) but I'd never had my own money before. And, although I missed my mum, I was enjoying being there. But the novelty soon wore off for reality took hold when the Mother told us we had chores to do.

'You have to make your bed every morning and, after school and on the weekend, you must polish the floors,' she told us, handing me a pinny. 'And I will be inspecting your work, so if it's not right then you'll do it again.'

I was shell-shocked. My own mum didn't do chores, never mind me! Disgruntled, I started to dislike this Mother. I knew she had our best interests at heart but I was desperate to see my own mum.

One day, I was polishing the floor when I suddenly stood up. I don't know what came over me but I just ran outside and in the direction of my gran's house; I didn't even whip my pinny off.

I ran what must have been two or three miles.

'What the...?!' spluttered Gran as I came flying through the door, coughing, spluttering and out of breath.

'I wanted to see Mum,' I gasped.

But when I saw her laid up in bed in the front room I panicked that she was poorly.

'She's fine,' soothed Gran. 'She's just had some teeth out so she's feeling a bit rotten.'

My aunty Rose took me back but I don't remember Mother being angry with me.

'Just don't do it again,' she gently warned me.

As time went on, I missed Mum even more. I never saw our Pauline but I'd see Terry when we played out; it was Mum I wanted to be at home with, though. She and Dad were allowed to visit us once a month and, each time they came, together, I asked when we would be allowed home.

'Soon,' said Mum. 'We're trying to get a house.'

I loved all the luxury in the cottages, but it came at a price and, as the months rolled on, I was becoming increasingly miserable and began to dislike the Mother of the House more and more. Perhaps there was a tinge of jealousy about it. You see, it was clear that Sylvia was her favourite; Mother made it quite obvious. It hadn't been the case at the beginning, but, the longer we were there, the more it started to develop. And, in fairness to Sylvia, I didn't blame her – I'd have lapped it up, too. She was two years younger than me, so perhaps Mother thought she was more vulnerable. But I was still only 12.

In July 1949 our cottage was taken to Fleetwood for a camping holiday. It was brilliant! We'd never been away on holiday before; instead, we'd just go to the park for the day. Of course, Mum and Dad couldn't afford it. But the Mother said she'd kit Sylvia and me out with some summer clothes. As we rummaged through those trunks, I'd never seen so many clothes – pretty ones at that – in my life! Seeing a cute summer dress, I pulled it out and told the Mother I wanted that one.

'No, not for you,' she replied, snatching it off me. 'You try it on, Sylvia.'

I was heartbroken and, the minute we arrived back, the next day after school, I ran to my gran's.

'I want to come *home!*' I sobbed, hugging Mum.

Thankfully, I didn't have to wait long until my wish was granted. Two months later, in September 1949, Sylvia and me were re-united with Terry, Pauline and Pat and taken home. I was buzzing with happiness that we were a complete family again. We never had anything, but I loved my family and we all got on.

As Mum opened the door to our new home on Brother Street, the smell of polish instantly became a distant memory, albeit one I'd secretly cherish for the rest of my life!

CHAPTER FOURTEEN

Starting Over

Our new home was like a palace compared to the previous ones. The only downside was the fact it was on the other side of town so I missed my friends from the old street as it was a couple of bus rides away and too far to go back to. I suppose that was a small price to pay for getting out of the old house, though.

It had three bedrooms and a bathroom, a luxury in itself, although still no carpets or lino on the wooden floors, but there was less damp. Mum told us it was one of the newer council houses and, although she paid rent, I didn't have the foggiest how much it cost to live there.

We had sheets, blankets and pillowcases on the beds – something unheard of before – and the living room had a three-piece suite and a built-in cupboard with drawers. But we lived mainly in the kitchen, which had a square table with four chairs, and two more beside the coal fireplace. We had an oven, but the fire had a back boiler, so it made the house warmer and for the first time ever we had hot running water. Heaven! I had no idea where all the furniture came from and it wasn't as if Mum would ever say. We had a back and a front garden, and the toilet was just outside the back door – no more running down the backyard in the freezing cold. I felt like royalty!

So, Sylvia, Pat, Pauline and me were in one room at the back, with our Sylvia and me sharing a bed and the younger two in another one. Our Terry was in the box room, which was the smallest of the three bedrooms, and Mum and Dad – who were now back together (I didn't ask how or why, I was just excited we were all back together) – were in the front bedroom.

I got on very well with my dad so I loved having him back at home. In fact, this is where I got my own back on our Sylvia for Dad used to take me – *just me* – to the pictures.

'It's always you, it's always you!' she sighed. He took me two or three times, but I don't know why it was just me.

'I know,' I replied smugly. I never questioned why because, if I'm being honest, I was having too much fun being the centre of attention for once. There were lots of picture houses in Blackburn then and I couldn't tell you how much it cost, but it was seen as a big treat to go.

A year later, Mum and Dad must have been getting on better because, when I was 14, my sister Marilyn was born in 1950. Being that bit older I was obviously more aware of a new baby coming into the house and I was very excited about it. Back then, women had their children at home so Mum's bed had been moved downstairs into the front room. One night I'd gone to bed as normal, and in the morning I got up to find I had a new sister! I'd not heard a thing but Mum had had her in the night, and now the little thing was sleeping soundly in the cot beside her. Dad was standing in front of the fire warming his behind and he just said, 'You better have a look – it's another one of you lot!' The way he said this, in such a matter-of-fact way, made us all giggle.

Mum never went to the hospital but, being the eldest girl, I was very hands-on – I even stayed off school for the first week of Marilyn's life to help Mum, who was still too sore to move about. I even got a letter from the school complaining that I'd been off, but I think Mum just shrugged because I was needed at home. In those days, family came first: with Dad out earning – just doing odd jobs here and there – I was the one to help out. And in a year's time, when I reached 15, I'd be leaving school and starting work anyhow. In fact, I often thought about where I'd end up. The mill was the obvious choice but I didn't want to think about it just yet. Thanks to Marilyn, our family seemed to be more settled and there was a happy vibe in the house.

In July of that same year, Mum sprang it on us that we were going to Blackpool for the day during Wakes Week. I was over the moon!

'*Really?*' I gasped. '*Honestly?* We are really going?'

'Yes,' she smiled. 'But only for the day, mind.'

'I don't care if it's for two hours!' I shrieked.

Wakes Week was the annual holiday for workers – and the highlight of the year for most of them. Back in the day, they only got one week, but in my time I'd only ever known it as two weeks and for us, in our town, it was always the last two weeks of July. Most of the town – well, those who could afford it, anyhow – went to the seaside town of Blackpool, about 40 minutes away by train. I'd heard kids at school talking about going and I always felt a pang of jealousy as we'd never been. No surprise that the night before I could hardly sleep with excitement.

'I'm going to go on the Big Dipper,' I whispered to Sylvia in bed. 'It's a roller-coaster and I've heard it's so scary!'

'I can't believe we're going to see the sea,' she replied. 'I hope Mum takes us to the beach.'

The next morning, I was up with the lark, ready for our trip. Mum packed us up some corned beef and cheese and onion sandwiches; we had a bottle of pop each too. We walked down to Cherry Tree station, just five minutes from our house, to catch the train to the Central Station in Blackpool. Already there were a few people on the platform, and with each stop the train got busier. A lot of them had suitcases because they must have been going for a few days, but I wasn't envious because to me just one day felt like a holiday.

'Here you go,' said Mum, giving us all half a crown. 'You can spend it on what you want but, once it's gone, that's it.'

The day was getting even better!

Mum and Dad (when they were together) always made sure we had days out to the park, but this was our first trip away, and I was so excited I thought I might burst.

'Can we go to the Pleasure Beach?' I asked.

'You can go where you like,' she smiled, nodding.

Once we'd arrived, Mum walked us all to the beach and said we'd stay there for a bit, have dinner and then walk to the Pleasure Beach. The beach was heaving, with kids playing in the sand, paddling and enjoying donkey rides. By then, Dad had already sloped off to the pub but we didn't mind and Mum never said anything. Once we'd gobbled down our butties we walked the few miles along the prom towards the Pleasure Beach. But I didn't care about the length of the walk because on the way there was so much to see, like the busy arcades and the little stalls selling gimmicky 'kiss me quick' hats and sticks of rock.

'I love it here!' I sighed as the Pleasure Beach grew closer and closer. Faced with the Big Dipper, which believe it or not is still there today, the Fun House, the Flying Machines (the oldest and most original ride in the park) and Noah's Ark, I didn't know what to go on first.

I spent hours in the theme park going on as many rides as I could before trying my luck on the penny machines in the arcades. And when my pockets were empty, with a heavy but happy heart, I knew it was time for us all to walk the few miles back up to the station to catch our train home.

'Let's get our photo taken,' I said to Sylvia, as we passed a photo booth. We didn't have a camera; it wasn't something we could afford. Sadly, we had no pictures of any of us as babies.

'Wow!' we giggled. I think that was the first photo we'd had of us together.

When we arrived at the train station, you should have seen my face drop when our Sylvia bought an ice cream! Unlike our Terry and me, she hadn't spent all her money at the Pleasure Beach, and as I looked longingly towards Mum, hoping she might take pity on me, she just sighed and said, 'Well, you've spent yours.'

To this day, I'm not sure how Mum and Dad managed to take us to Blackpool, but it was a happy day that became a tradition and carried on for a few more years. I only stopped going once I was married.

The next morning, once home and back to reality, Mum sent me to the butcher's for a 'five-bob-lap-up' – it was sausages, a piece of meat (a shoulder), corned beef, mincemeat and a piece of brawn, all for five shillings. We bought it from Frank Pennell, a butcher in the Whalley Range area (he later moved to Blackburn Market), near to where Grandma lived. I used to go every Saturday morning and it would take ages as I had to walk and catch a bus. It was great, especially in winter. The meat would last us all a week because Mum made stews and soups to keep us fed.

Mum and Dad were getting along just fine. To be honest, they always did ... until drink was involved. On Saturday nights, they'd go to the pub together and I'd babysit. This was nothing new to me as I'd been doing it for years. Mum always drank half pints of beer and Dad would drink a pint.

I'd dread them coming home as that was when the rows began. Usually, I'd scarper up the stairs to bed the minute they came through the door. And once I was tucked up in bed their voices would get louder and louder. Dad was never violent – he just wasn't a happy drunk, drink made him crazy.

Anyhow, I didn't mind babysitting. After all, it wasn't as if I had any money to go out. And then, on a Sunday, I'd go to Corporation Park – where my parents met – where there'd be a gang of us. It was innocent fun as we played games like hide and seek and kiss chase, when we weren't on the swings. And on other nights my friends and me would go round each other's houses. On the rare occasion when I had some money (not very often), I went to the pictures.

When I was 14, a lad from around the corner called Kenneth asked if I wanted to go to the pictures with him.

'I don't want to,' I told Mum.

Kenneth was a nice lad, but he was quiet and wore glasses so I suppose I thought he was a bit of a nerd. I wasn't interested in boys in a romantic sense and, even if I had been, then he certainly wasn't doing anything for me, but Mum made me go.

'He's had the decency to knock on the front door and ask you, so you're going!' she ordered.

I had a nice night and Kenneth, bless him, walked me home too, like all the boys and men did in those days. Sadly, though, as I said, I wasn't interested in boys, and especially not him.

Although there was a mixed gang of us who hung out on the park and a few boys on our street, we were just friends. I was at Bangor School and boys and girls were not only in separate classes but also in different parts of the school so it wasn't as if you mixed with them there.

I enjoyed school, apart from when we had to attend the nit clinic every six months to see the nit nurse, who we called 'Nitty Nora'. The clinic was in town so that meant we had to walk there. Going there wasn't the problem but 'Nora' poured white powder onto my mousey hair before giving my head a thorough inspection. The blasted stuff stayed in your hair, meaning I had to walk back to school with everyone knowing where I'd been. It was so humiliating!

Other days, we went swimming, which I loved. And on the way back to school, we always stopped off at a cake shop.

With Mum having no money, I was given free dinners and I always remember I didn't care what it was – I was so hungry I wolfed it down. The only thing I turned my nose up at was the marmalade pudding.

I was never good in classes as I wasn't academic, but I used to enjoy the home economics lessons. Basically, they taught you how to be a wife – something unheard of today! We learned how to make a bed, to cook and sew, and I thought it was brilliant, much more interesting than silly maths. I loved the cooking classes the best, though, especially as it meant I could eat what I'd made. Mum would have to give me the ingredients and we'd bake pies and cakes, the idea being to then take them home. If I ever made a dozen of something, I'd stuff six down me before I got home.

'All that stuff I gave you and you've only made this!' Mum tutted.

'Yes,' I nodded, without feeling one ounce of guilt.

As I've said, I wasn't interested in academic lessons. I liked history but I was rubbish at maths, and always getting in trouble for one reason or another. My problem was that I just wanted to have fun. I suppose I was a little mischievous (something I'd carry on being in later life!) but it was harmless and I was only being a kid.

Somehow my dad ended up as caretaker of the school. And me being me, I hadn't thought about this when I decided to take a girl's fountain pen. At the time, I wasn't being nasty, I just saw something I'd never be able to have for myself, so I took it. The girl told the teacher it was me who'd stolen her pen so he asked if it was true. Without thinking, I replied, 'No, it's mine. My dad gave it to me.'

I was sent to the headmistress, and she went and fetched my dad.

'I never gave it to ya,' he said.

Well, I never stole again – apart from the time when Mum sent me to the corner shop just off my street and I spotted a dish of walnuts on the shelf. Looking around, I saw the shopkeeper wasn't there and so I took one. No sooner had I got it in my hand than a voice boomed, 'Put that back or I'm going to tell your mother!' It was the shopkeeper, who could see me from behind the curtain.

So, I never stole again (apart from those two times) because I had to stay behind after school and then walk home – a journey that would usually take me two buses. When I eventually got home, tired and hungry, I was dreading a clout from Mum, but instead I just got a telling off from Dad.

'What you telling lies for?' he asked.

But I just shrugged. In fairness, I don't think it was a telling off, more of a question, which I didn't have an answer for. I never did it again, though.

School was different in those days and certainly not like today. I don't remember doing any exams and we didn't have aspirations, unlike girls today. As I was approaching my 15th birthday, my thoughts turned to what I'd do when I left school.

I remember a conversation I had with my mum around this time: 'I don't want to go in mill with you and our Marie,' I told her. 'It looks horrid in there and you're always so tired and dirty.'

Mum had started to work in Bank Mill, in an area called Cherry Tree, just five minutes' walk from our house. The mill was on the north side of the Leeds and Liverpool Canal and had been open since 1865. She'd been in there for a few years before and after having our Marilyn. A piecer in the spinning shed, she had two and a half frames. She never moaned about the work, but I know it was tiring because she was on her feet all day. Her job was to tie together the broken yarn on a spinning mule. On the huge, moving machine, it required nimble fingers and quick feet, especially as she was on piece rates, which meant she was paid in relation to how much work she did.

The conditions in her department were dreadful; temperatures had to be kept high and humid to prevent the thread from breaking and cotton dust hung in the air; often it was inhaled. I don't recall Dad ever working in the mill but that might have been because he already had a bad chest and the conditions there would have made it even worse.

'Well, what else you going to do?' she said.

Although working in the mill was the obvious choice for a girl of my age and ability, not everyone went in – I knew some of my friends from school had gone to work in a shop.

'Don't know,' I replied, 'but anything other than that mill!'

I'd seen how hard Mum worked. Always she came home filthy and shattered. She worked from 7.30am to 5.30pm, with an hour for dinnertime and just two 10-minute breaks – one in the morning and the other in the afternoon. Although she didn't seem to mind it, it was so strenuous. Each night, Sylvia and me helped make tea and we always did the washing up. To me it just seemed like a hard job and, to be honest, I wanted something easier.

I'd also seen how dangerous the mill could be through our Terry, who worked at Cherry Tree Mill, opposite the one where Mum worked. He worked in the card room and he was only 17, so he couldn't have been there more than two years. Carding is the mechanical process that disentangles and cleans the fibre so it's ready to spin. The carding machine consists of one big roller surrounded by smaller ones. All of the rollers are covered in small teeth and, as the cotton progresses further on, the teeth get finer. The cotton leaves the carding machine in the form of a sliver, a large rope of fibres.

Anyhow, I'm not sure what he did that day, but something off the machine flew out and cut his bottom lip off and knocked his front teeth out. When I came home from school, poor Terry was in bed.

'What's up?' I asked Mum. 'Is he poorly?'

'He got his teeth knocked out and lost part of his lip in mill,' she replied.

Terry had been to hospital. They'd stitched part of his lip back on and he'd lost his front teeth but they were never replaced. The poor boy looked a right mess and back in the day it wasn't as if there was any insurance or sick pay. Terry was off work for a week but Mum couldn't afford him to be off any longer because he wasn't bringing any money in.

As I left his room and came down for tea, I remember thinking the mill wasn't for me. Not only was it hard work, it could be a death trap too. I knew I was being over-dramatic but I didn't want my teeth knocked out, like poor Terry. And what if something hit my face? I wanted somewhere I could have a bit of fun and to me the mill sounded as if that was the last place it was possible.

A year later, when Terry was 18, he was called up to do National Service for two years. He was posted to Preston and then overseas to Aden, in Egypt, but returned to the mill once he had finished.

Now, back then, you left school in either July, Christmas or Easter, depending when you reached 15. So, with my birthday being in November, I knew I could finish at Christmas. A mate of mine had told me there were jobs going at Newman's Footwear Ltd., a slipper factory in Blackburn where she worked (around 1960, the company progressed from slippers to ladies' and children's fashion shoes).

A big employer, it had about 500 staff. Their main factory was based at Griffin Works in Stancliffe Street and was five storeys tall. But my job was at the factory at Brookhouse, close to the area of Blackburn called Little Harwood. There was no interview then, I just went along and spoke to the manager, who confirmed there was a job available and I could start in the New Year.

Counting down the last few weeks of school, I couldn't wait to leave. On my last day, I stood at the gates and smiled with relief at the thought I'd never have to go back there again. I don't think I even bothered taking any tests – there was no point. But I soon realised school was a doddle compared to work and found myself wishing I was back there.

Christmas came and went, and in January 1952 I was excited about starting work. Mum was working in the mill so she'd always be up early and made sure us kids were awake before she left, not long after 7am. I started work at 8am so that day Mum came in and made sure I was awake. She didn't want me to be late on my first day and knew it was a bit of a trek for me to get to work since I needed to catch two buses.

'Come on, get up,' she said. 'Now, have a good day and just do as you're told.'

'Yeah, all right,' I replied sleepily.

After pulling on my pencil skirt and blouse, I slipped on my ballerina pumps (a popular shoe, they were called 'flatties' and had a half-inch heel or none at all, black being a common colour with a thin bow on top), and off I went.

'Good luck!' shouted Sylvia.

When I arrived at the factory, a middle-aged man (the manager) led me to a big room, where I had a workstation to myself.

'You have to staple the corners of the cardboard to make the box,' he explained. Although pleasant enough, I didn't really think anything of him.

I was to be paid £2 and 10 shillings a week. Five shillings went towards my stamp and insurance, £2 to my mum and I got five shillings for myself, which would be about 25 pence in today's money.

I enjoyed work, but I enjoyed having money in my pocket more; it meant I could go out! Also, I was really grateful not to be in the mills. Around this time, I started to go to

Kenzita's dance hall every Saturday night. Situated just by the *Telegraph* (the newspaper) office in the boulevard, it was where we were taught how to ballroom dance. I loved going there and, on a Sunday, I'd show Mum my moves in the living room.

'You can move,' she said. 'I just hope you don't dance too close to boys like that.'

'Mum!' I shrieked, laughing.

Mum and I got on great, and she often teased me. She was such a character and full of life. We might not have had much and at most times nothing but Mum always made us feel loved and we had a lot of laughs. I could tell her anything too. I'd never have crossed or messed with her, though. Indeed, up until she passed away in 2012, aged 94, I still didn't answer her back.

And it was at Kenzita's that I not only had my first waltz but my first taste of romance too.

Back then, a girl would stand or sit and wait for a boy to come over and ask her to dance. And, if you were lucky, he might even ask if he could walk you home. I'd had a few dances with different boys, but they all felt like nothing more than a friend until I danced with Alan Powdrill.

It was July 1952 and I was 15 years old. When he came over to ask me to dance, my heart did a flutter. With his blond locks and shy but welcoming smile, I thought he was lovely.

'He's so nice!' I swooned to my friends.

Alan was 18 and, like our Terry, doing National Service. As he waltzed me around the floor, I was floating on air. So, was this what everyone talked about? Was I in love? We met every Saturday and courted for a month. In reality, we only saw each other three times, but I was heartbroken when he told me he was to be posted to Aden, near Egypt for a few months as part of his National Service.

'I'll write,' he promised.

I can't remember how many letters we wrote back and forth, but a few weeks later, when he told me that his mother wanted to meet me, I shrieked with delight.

'You know what that means?' said our Sylvia.

'It can't be!' I cried. 'Do you think he's going to propose, Mum?'

'Could be,' she smiled.

In those days, women were desperate to be married by the age of 18 or 19. Like everyone else, the last thing Mum wanted was for me to be left on the shelf – that's why she'd encouraged me to go to the pictures with Kenneth that time.

All week, I had knots in my stomach as I waited for Sunday to come round. It seemed everything was falling into place: I had a job

I liked and a boyfriend who might become my fiancé! And, if things couldn't get any better, that morning Mum suddenly handed me a new red gabardine mac.

'You needed a new one,' she said.

In fairness, she was right, as I'd been wearing my navy one since I started school and it was literally falling to bits. But I was overwhelmed that Mum had bought this one for me. Well, she would have got it 'on the tick', meaning she'd be paying off the 39 shillings and 11 pence (£2.00 in today's money) for a long time, but I knew she'd think it was worth it. We might have been poor but she was proud and wanted me to look presentable.

'Ooh, I do feel posh!' I gushed, as I did a little twirl.

'Go on, get going,' she smiled, shooing me out the door. 'You don't want to be late.'

My skinny bones chattered all the way on the bus to Oswaldtwistle, a town 12 miles from Blackburn. Alan's house was just a typical two up, two down. As the door opened, a small, slim woman welcomed me with a smile and invited me to come in. It was Alan's mum and she led me straight to the parlour, which was another word for the front room, and I could smell a roast cooking from the kitchen. The room was nicer than ours at home; it was cleaner and they had a few more bits of furniture.

I could hear voices in there so I assumed it was Alan's father and his sister (although I never saw them) and, with that, his mother reappeared and handed me a brew and a lettuce sandwich.

I felt so uncomfortable I wanted to get up and run away. His mother was pleasant enough but I couldn't believe she'd brought me a sandwich when clear as day they were having a Sunday roast! After about 10 minutes I made some excuse and left, feeling mortified all the way home on the bus. On arrival, I told Mum what had happened.

'They did *what?*' she fumed.

'They just left me with a lettuce sandwich and cup of tea as they had their Sunday lunch,' I repeated.

Mum may have been poor but she was proud and would never have treated anyone the same way I'd been treated. In an instant, she was put off by Alan and his mum – I knew she thought I could do better.

Now, everyone knew a mother's approval was vital, so I waited anxiously for the next few days, swooning over the black and white photo of Alan wearing his khaki uniform. Finally, a week later, a letter arrived from him.

'Oh, no!' I cried, reading the letter. 'How can she not like me?'

Alan had written that his mother hadn't liked me and, because of that, he couldn't see me anymore.

'You're better off without him,' comforted Mum. 'He sounds like a mummy's boy.'

There was no reason or explanation but that was it and I never saw or heard from Alan again. Heartbroken, I cried like a baby.

'It will be OK,' soothed Mum.

But it felt as if my world had ended so I was grateful to at least have a job that I enjoyed. And I liked it at the slipper place – I'd been there a few months by then and, although I worked mainly by myself, I'd got to know a lot of the other workers too. At break time or lunch, we'd often have a laugh and a gossip.

A few days later, I was still feeling down in the dumps. I'd told my work colleagues that Alan had finished with me because of his mother.

'Silly bugger!' said some.

'Plenty more fish in the sea,' added others.

They were a great crowd and at least work took my mind off my troubles. There was always a lot going on in the packing room, where I worked. In the middle of the room was a conveyor belt where all the boxes were put on and then packed with the smaller ones ready for delivery.

This one lunchtime, as usual, we were having a laugh and a joke with some of the lads in the room, when suddenly one of them got hold of me, lifted me up and put me inside one of the empty bigger boxes on the conveyor belt as a joke. So, I was going around the conveyor belt, head peeking out from the box, and the whole floor – including me – was in hysterics. Suddenly, a voice boomed from the doorway: 'What are you doing in *there?*'

My heart sank when I recognised the foreman's voice.

'I'm just having a ride,' I replied, a little sheepish.

'Get out!' he shouted. 'Get to the office. *Now!*'

As I stumbled out of the box, suddenly the giggles were replaced by shushes and whispers as I scurried, eyes down, to the office. My cheeks were the colour of our very own Lancashire rose.

I was sacked on the spot and I can't say I blame them. After all, I was mucking about and it did look as if it was my entire fault, but the last thing I was going to do was tell tales, so I took my punishment and walked out. On the way home, I was more worried about how I'd explain it all to Mum than anything else.

'You've *what?*' she cried.

'I've been sacked,' I mumbled.

But, instead of a clout or a telling off, Mum just laughed when I explained why.

'So, it wasn't really my fault,' I told her.

Mum simply shook her head and smirked. 'Well, you know where you're going, young lady,' she said.

'Oh, no!' I sighed.

'You're in the mill on Monday,' she told me. 'I'll see the foreman.'

In those days, there was no such thing as a reference. You'd come out of one job and into another – I was just gutted that job happened to be the mill.

So, I'd lost the love of my life (well, that's how it seemed at the time) and I'd also been sacked. Could life get any worse?

CHAPTER FIFTEEN

The Dreaded Mill

That Monday morning, in August 1952 when I was 15, accompanied by Mother, I dragged my heels all the way to the mill. 'I can't do it!' I sulked. She sighed and shook her head. My heart sank. Of course, I'd seen the mill hundreds of times before, but now it was different – now, I was going in. I'd never seen a place so depressing; I wanted to cry.

From our house, the mill was a five-minute walk. And that morning, as we walked through the yard towards the big, dingy-looking building, I was dreading the day that lay ahead. I had plenty of mates from school already working there, and then my mum and my aunties Marie and Dot, so I was aware that the place was two storeys, with just a winding and spinning room. Now, as I saw it for myself, the thought of being stuck in there depressed me. And, as Mum led me through towards the office and the smell of oil from the machines stung the back of my throat, I was already desperate to leave.

'I'm not staying in mill all time!' I moaned.

It was filthy.

'You'll stay in as long as I say, as it looks like I need to keep my eye on ya!' Mum insisted.

Mum introduced me to the personnel person, who was in the small, basic office. 'You can put her in with us,' she suggested. Mum was a spinner so that meant I'd be on the first floor (the winding shed was always on the top floor because of the weight of the machinery).

'Right, she can be a doffer then,' he replied.

No one explained to me what a doffer was but, because our Dot did it, I kind of had some idea. Doffer means 'to take off', so, as the bobbins on the spinning frame filled with thread (these were known as 'cones'), it would be my job to replace them with empty ones (also known as cones).

I followed Mum into a huge room full of spinning frames, where there must have been about 16 of them, each with hundreds of bobbins on either side of the frame, known as 'two sides'.

'Stand here,' she told me, as she called Dot over.

'We're supposed to keep walking up and down to check the frames but, once one is full, they'll shout for us,' explained Dot.

No training, we just got on with it – I supposed we learned on the job.

'What, *all* day?' I sighed. 'And *all* the machines?'

There were six doffers in total and they were all about my age. I knew them from school and around the area, but before I could even have a chat with any of them the machines started up and I'd never heard a racket like it.

'Oh, my goodness!' I cried, covering up my ears in the hope that I could shut out the horrendous noise.

'That's why you lip read,' mouthed Dot.

'*What?*' I mouthed back.

I knew this work would take some getting used to! Soon, we were being shouted at, so I followed Dot to a frame to watch her pull off the full bobbin and put on a new one. I may have been apprehensive about the work but one thing I wasn't worried about was being cold in there! The climate was a little chilly outside, but, no sooner had the machines fired up and with me walking up and down, I soon became warm. As the morning went on, I'd never been so thankful when Dot mee-mawed (the mill workers' form of miming) the drinks sign to me.

'Brew time,' she mouthed.

Now I understood *that!*

Because the noise was so intense, the language of the mill was not spoken but to mime, and of course lip read. But they didn't stop the machines. Oh, no! Instead, you took it in turns to run to the kettle with your mug and make a quick brew.

'Any milk?' I asked our Dot.

'No,' she replied. 'You drink it black.'

Milk would have gone off in a place like that, what with the warm temperature and of course this was before the days of canteens so we didn't have a fridge or anything like that to store it. Oh, and it tasted horrible, it did, but that didn't stop anyone drinking it as we were always gasping for a brew.

By lunchtime, I was hot and exhausted when I met up with my pals, Mavis Barnes and Dorothy Woodcocks. Mavis had ginger hair and was a nice girl; she was a winder (they would wind thread on bobbins that came up from the spinning room). Dorothy was a doffer like me, and, oh, she was bonny! I knew them from the area; we went to Kenzita's together and round each other's houses. The same age as me, they had been working in the mill a few months as they'd joined straight from leaving school.

The three of us sat on the fire escape in the fresh air to eat our corned beef sandwiches. I never questioned why I was a doffer and Mavis was a winder, but I knew a doffer was the job most people started on in the mill and something like a spinner, which Mother did, required someone with more experience. Anyhow, what Mum did looked far harder so I was quite happy doffing for the time being.

'You get used to it,' Dorothy smiled.

'It's so noisy,' I said.

'I know,' replied Mavis.

'And dirty,' I added. Already the pinny that I was wearing over my skirt and blouse was full of oil and it had to last me all week. 'Yet you, Dorothy, look spick and span!'

'I don't know about that!' she laughed.

But she did, and from that day on I always thought she did, unlike me. By the end of the day, I looked as if I'd been down the mine, never mind the mill.

With that, a few other women came to sit with us. They were probably about my mum's age. After that first day, I always sat outside when it was nice but in winter we'd just sit at the end of the spinning room. All the women would mix, and some days I'd sit with my mum and others my pals. As they tucked into their sandwiches, they began to talk freely about what they'd been up to that weekend.

'We spent most of it rowing,' said one, talking about her husband. 'He's a piggin' a*****e!'.

With that the other women fell into a fit of giggles as my jaw dropped open with shock.

'She swore,' I whispered to Mavis and Dorothy.

'You'll get used to the language in here

too,' they smiled. 'They're always effing and blinding!'

Now don't get me wrong, I wasn't that innocent, but I'd never heard proper swearing before. Mum and Dad used to say 'bloody' and 'bugger' all the time but I think it was the surprise of hearing older women, in public, use stronger language so blatantly, without care! I don't know if I was more shocked about hearing a lady swear or the fact that the other two didn't look at all fazed and were laughing. But, as each of the women took turns to moan about her husband, I began to understand that for them the mill was their solace. It was their place to let off steam and gossip with their mates. And as they laughed like teenagers I suddenly saw something special about the mill: friendship.

By 5.30pm, all the machines had been switched off. I was dead on my feet and had never felt so exhausted in all my life.

'Thank goodness that's over with,' I sighed to Mum as we walked out of the building into the fresh air, my ears still ringing but grateful for the peace and quiet. 'I'm ready for bed.'

'Chance'll be a fine thing!' she smirked.

Our working day may have ended but we still had to go home, help make tea and wash up. On the short walk home, I told Mum about the other women's language.

'That's what they're like,' she laughed. 'You'll have to get used to that!'

Back home, I felt grubby but I knew that I wouldn't be able to have a bath for another six days, being that Sunday was bath night. Mum always filled up the tin bath with water heated from the fire and we had a wash. But it wasn't a luxury, unlike the time in the cottage home, as Sylvia and me would usually share the water and the soap would be the block of Fairy soap we had and it didn't smell half as nice.

As I've said, my pinny was already filthy but there was no chance I'd get it washed before the end of the week (or have the money to have two of them) as nothing was ever washed before then. Sunday morning was washing day and I hated it. Mum washed everything by hand in the dolly tub by scrubbing the Fairy block of soap onto each garment and then it'd be mine and Sylvia's job to rinse and hang them outside if it was nice, or they'd dry on a rack over the fire in the kitchen. There would be piles of washing strewn around the house and it was such a long, boring chore, I hated it. By Sunday morning, the house was covered in dirty laundry, thanks to us five kids just whipping off our clothes and not caring where they were flung, knowing Mum would pick them all up on wash day.

And as I crawled into bed at 10pm after my

first day in the mill, I don't think I ever slept as well. As I reflected back, there was no disputing that working in the mill was a long and tiring job (it got even worse in winter, when we started and left work in the dark), but even after my short time in there it was plain to see that the friendship and camaraderie in the place was what got you through the day.

And just a few days in, although I still didn't like my job, oddly enough I was settling into the mill and starting to feel at home there purely because I knew a lot of people working there. From day one, I had people coming over to say hello and ask how I was getting on. And don't forget, I had Mum and my two aunties working in there plus a couple of mates, so for me it was more of a social gathering than work, and that was great. As I've said, I got on really well with my mum and, with my aunties not being that much older than me, they were friends too. Today, I doubt there are many jobs where you can all work together like that.

So, by Friday, I'd settled in and by then I'd also got to know a few more of the other women and already had some of the others sussed out.

One of the spinners was called Sissy and she was the kindest, sweetest woman in there. A married lady, I think she had children and

I'd say she was in her 50s. She'd not say boo to a goose but would always ask me what I'd been up to at the weekend, or what I was planning on doing the coming one.

'You going out dancing this weekend, Maureen?' she'd ask, as we all sat around on Friday lunchtime.

'Yes,' I'd reply. 'I'm off to Kenzita's – I love it!'

'Ooh, me too!' she gushed. 'I used to love dancing but don't get to do it these days, not like you young 'uns.'

On the other hand, there was Maggie-Anne and she was a tyrant. A biggish, older woman, she was a spinner too and we used to joke about how she could manage to fit between the looms, though never to her face as we were frightened to death of her. She was right bad-tempered and always moaning about one thing or another – mainly about us doffers.

'We're flogging our hearts out and them young 'uns are just standing there,' she'd fume.

And, if we ever back-chatted her, she went mad. She was married and, although into her 60s and well past retirement age, she couldn't afford to stop working. There were a few women in there who were the same, but it was nothing unusual, for people simply couldn't afford not to work. Looking back, no wonder she was bad-tempered, having to work at that age, and it didn't help us rascals winding her up.

That afternoon, I spotted a few of the women patting their bottoms.

'What's that for?' I asked Dot.

'It's our wage,' she mouthed back. 'It's to let people know he is here.'

I wondered why everyone had suddenly cheered up!

There was a man standing by a machine handing over the wages to the workers. I got £2 and 10 shillings, like the slipper factory, so I split my wage the same way as before. And, as I ripped open the pay packet and counted my coins, suddenly that first week in the mill hadn't been all that bad. OK, I didn't like the awful conditions – the fact that I was covered in oil, forever sweating because of the heat and my ears were constantly ringing due to the noise – but I liked the people.

I soon found that I had to pick up lip reading, otherwise I was going to struggle in there.

'It'll come soon enough,' said Mum, when I confided in her. 'It's the only way to communicate in there so you have to learn it!'

Now, I can't remember how long it took me to learn, and it's funny, at the time I never thought I would, but I soon did. Like anything in life, I was doing it before I realised without even thinking.

I worked with women of all ages and characters. At that stage, I didn't have much to do with the men in the mill as most of them were maintenance workers, who were only called over by some of the women if they had trouble with their machine. I'd catch the odd one having a bit of a flirt with a woman as he fixed her machine, but if one ever caught my eye I'd drop my head with embarrassment. I was far too shy to talk to an older man!

One thing I'd learned early on was the laughter. While the machines were running that's all you'd hear, but the minute everyone broke for lunch it would start. There was a lot of banter in the mills and you soon had to get involved. But as well as the banter came support and, if anyone was ever upset or had some bad news, the women rallied round.

A few months after I'd been there, our Dot came in, looking upset.

'Are you all right? What's up?' I asked, concerned. We'd only just hung up our coats so the machines hadn't started yet and we were able to talk.

'It's Uncle Arthur,' said Dot. 'He's dead – he died last night at home.'

My uncle Arthur was blind but I don't remember him being ill or my grandma nursing him, so it must have been sudden.

At the time I wasn't surprised as he was 70 and, unlike now, that was considered old. I was broken-hearted as he was the first person to have an impact on me when he'd died, being old enough to understand. Mum was upset too, but, as I didn't work close to her and she had to get on, a few of the other women gave me a much-needed hug while I had a little weep.

'He couldn't see so he used to sit in the same spot all day beside the fire and we would wind him up by pulling his jumper or poking his ear with a twig and take the mickey out of him. He'd always shout back, waving his walking stick, 'Who's that? I'll get you, you little buggers!'

'Sounds like a character,' soothed one.

'He was,' I smiled.

'Then it would be a sadder day if tears weren't falling for him,' another told me.

A few days later, I was allowed to have the day off to attend his funeral but I had to take it as unpaid leave, as did Mum (the mill owner would only pay you for the day if the deceased was a direct relative). But I didn't care – I was just relieved to be able to have the day off to say my goodbye.

The solidarity of the women was unique: family or not, they all looked out for each other because in there you were a community. I remember one day, I was crippled over with period pain and one of the older women stepped away from her machine to see if I was OK.

'You al'reet?' she asked.

I'd started my periods when I was 14, and at the time I was in my cookery class at school. It was a shock because I didn't know what was happening as it wasn't something I ever discussed with my mum or even my friends. Mum never had the birds and the bees talk with me, it just wasn't the done thing, and, if I'm honest, my friends and me didn't talk about it either as we were all frightened of what happened. I remember going to see the headmistress, who handed me a piece of string and a big, thick sanitary towel with two loops attached. I'd seen one before – perhaps at home, I wasn't sure – but I didn't know what to do.

'You put the sanitary towel in your underwear, put the string through the hoops and tie it up at the side,' she explained.

'Thank you,' I replied, blushing. The towel was so big and clumpy it felt like a brick between my legs and there was nothing exhilarating about the whole thing of finally becoming a woman. In fact, if that's what being a woman meant, they could stick it! It was a far cry from the sanitary towels of today and, of course, tampons hadn't even been invented.

That afternoon when I got home, I told

my mum what had happened.

'I thought you may have been as you looked awful white this morning,' she said. 'We don't have any towels so you'll have to go to the shop for some.'

But I knew the shopkeeper in our local shop was a man.

'I'm not going to ask for *them!*' I cried, mortified. 'I'm not going; I *can't!*'

Nowadays, no one thinks twice about buying sanitary protection – I even chuckle when I see men buying it for their partners, thinking how that wouldn't have happened in my day – but back then I remember being mortified at the thought. In the end, I think Mum had to go!

And, although it was still something you didn't discuss with men, the women in the mill were open with each other about their periods. So, that day when I was suffering from the pains, one woman (I can't remember her name) was asking if I was OK. I thought I'd have to suffer in silence, too embarrassed to admit what was wrong.

'Don't be daft, love,' she soothed. 'We all suffer the same, no need to be shy.' It was such a refreshing – and forward-thinking – attitude. 'Go and get some Indian brandy from the medical box and mix it with hot water,' she told me. 'That'll make you feel better, love.'

The camaraderie with the women in the

mill was amazing; they all looked out for each other and it made me realise just how strong women are.

Every Monday dinnertime, the women would quiz each other on their weekend and the younger ones especially would be asked if they'd been out with any lads.

'Eh, kid, did he walk you home?' one would ask. 'Did you give him a kiss?'

As the younger girls remained coy and bashful, the older ones would laugh but it was never in a nasty way, more because of their innocence and what was ahead of them, i.e. sex!

By Friday, the conversation had switched to what everyone was planning on doing that weekend.

'Are you going looking for lads?' the older women would tease me and the other girls who were off to the dances.

The women were so funny and had a way of saying things. They were really down-to-earth and their way of getting through the working day was by the friendships they formed in the mill. And, whenever someone got married or had a baby, a collection would go round: 'Come on, put ya hand in ya pocket!' they'd say. Some were a bit rough around the edges but you never back-chatted them – you had respect for the older women.

Another thing that they collected for in the

mill was to have your photo professionally taken. One dinnertime, a woman came round with a hat.

'What's that for?' I asked Mavis.

'It's to see who is next to have their photo taken,' she explained. 'You pay sixpence every week for twelve weeks and one gets picked out each week and that person goes to Leslie's to have it done. They keep going round until everyone has had it done and then it begins again.'

Leslie's was a photography shop at No. 40 Bank Top, not far from the mill.

'Oh, how fancy!' I gushed. I'd only ever had my picture taken in a booth on Blackpool front with our Sylvia but nothing this fancy, like film stars had.

'Can I have in?' I asked the woman with the hat.

'Course you can, love,' she smiled. 'We'll start again in couple of weeks.'

So, soon enough, when I got my wage I gave her sixpence, and when I'd reached six shillings – the cost of the photograph – twelve weeks later my name was put into the hat. In between chatting about the weekend, Friday lunchtime also became a regular spot for the photographer draw: 'Whose turn is it?' we'd all ask excitedly.

I can't remember how long I had to wait to be chosen but, in total, I think I went twice and I know Mavis came, too. Ooh, we thought we were the bee's knees as we sat on a stool in front of a black canvas and the photographer snapped away! We were pleased as punch, Mavis and me.

'You look beautiful, kid,' said the older women as we proudly showed off our pictures. We felt so grown up.

As well as forming some great friendships in the mill, I also got friendly with a girl called Eva Alberts, a pretty girl of mixed race, whom I met at Kenzita's. My failing memory these days means I can't remember where she worked but I know it wasn't in the mill – or not ours, anyhow. Eva lived on the way to Cherry Tree, not far from my house. Now, I thought we were poor but Eva was worse, bless her! Her house was worse than ours; it was dirty and horrible. Her mum had a house full of kids, though, so it was no wonder, and I'm not sure what her dad did for work or her mother for that matter. I remember there was no racism towards the family, considering her dad was black and had come over during the war, though.

Now, Eva and me, along with Mavis and Dorothy loved going to Kenzita's but at work I heard the older girls talking about the Tower Ballroom in Blackpool. It was the place anybody and everybody went to. So, not long after my 16th birthday in November 1952, Mavis, Dorothy and me were having dinner together one Friday in the mill when the subject was brought up.

'How about we go to the Tower tomorrow? Some of the girls from here are going,' suggested Mavis. 'We're all 16 now so I don't see why we can't go.'

(That tended to be the age girls started to go.)

My face must have lit up like the Illuminations.

'I'll have to ask my mum but I don't see why not,' I replied.

As we shrieked with joy at the thought, Maggie-Anne asked what all the carry-on was about.

'We're going to the Tower!' replied Dorothy.

'What, to pick up lads?' she smirked.

My cheeks turned crimson but I should have been used to the banter in there by then.

That afternoon, as I walked home with Mum, I asked her about the Tower.

'Who are you going with? How are you getting there?' she wanted to know.

I told her it was with Mavis, Dorothy and a few others from the mill, and I was going to ask Eva, too.

'OK,' she said, 'just be careful and stick together. I want you on that 11 o'clock train home, too!'

'Thanks, Mum!' I shrieked.

Mum was great – she trusted me so she never stopped me from going out. In fact, I used to walk home by myself from Kenzita's (something I'd never dream of doing today) but it was different back then.

Back home, I was like a giddy kipper counting the hours down to our trip to the Tower the next day.

'I wish I was going,' said Sylvia, as the pair of us washed up.

'I know,' I replied, 'but you'll soon be able to and in the meantime I promise to tell you all about it. I know it's going to change my life!'

At the time, I didn't realise how true that statement was going to be.

CHAPTER SIXTEEN

Becoming a Woman

After pulling on my stockings and suspenders, I slipped on a grey pencil skirt and fastened my elasticated waspa black belt around my waist. After being in curling pins all day, my mousey, shoulder-length hair had curled under nicely. Butterflies fluttered in my stomach as I ran down the wooden stairs and grabbed my smart red mac (the one Mum had bought me for my visit to Alan's house).

'You look nice,' said Sylvia.

'Thanks,' I smiled. 'Right, I'm off.'

'Have a good time,' said Mum, 'and stay together.'

As I ran down the hill towards Cherry Tree station to meet the others for the 6pm train to Blackpool, I couldn't believe we were finally going to the Tower. It was November 1952 and I felt like the happiest 16-year-old alive. Not even the cold, miserable weather could dampen my spirits.

'I can't wait!' I cried, handing over my half a crown to the conductor for a return ticket.

'Me too,' replied Mavis.

The train was packed with young people all heading our way. After pulling in at the station, it was only a short walk to the Tower.

'That's two shillings and sixpence,' said the doorman, as a queue of eager dancers filtered in.

'*Wow!*' I gasped at the huge and impressive ballroom. I'd never seen anything as magnificent in all my life, it was so stylish and charming. I felt so grown up and I couldn't wait to start dancing. Huge crystal chandeliers illuminated the wooden, sparkly floor (I'd never seen a floor so shiny!). Above the stage was the inscription (still there today): 'Bid me discourse, I will enchant thine ear' from the poem 'Venus and Adonis' by William Shakespeare.

To this day, the ballroom is still regarded as one of the country's premier dancing venues and now it's even more well known and popular, thanks to *Strictly Come Dancing* being hosted there.

As the organist Reginald Dixon, known affectionately as 'Mr Blackpool', played the Foxtrot, more people hit the floor. And, after I'd breathed in the ballroom's beauty, I soon realised how busy it was. There were no free tables or chairs and by now the floor was rammed.

'Come on,' said Eva, grabbing my arm as we fought through the crowd to the top end of the floor, where we stood and waited to be asked to dance.

And, as an RAF private approached and asked me to dance, my heart did a flutter.

'Go on,' nudged Eva, as he led me to the floor.

After a few dances, I'd built up a thirst but it wasn't as if we could go into the bar, or order an alcoholic drink. Through tittle-tattle at the mill, I'd heard stories about some girls (underage) going into one of the pubs around the corner from the Tower, where they got served as the landlord never asked for ID. But I didn't fancy that (and never did). Anyhow, my mum would have given me a good hiding if she'd smelled booze on my breath, or, worse still, if I were tipsy. Also, I didn't have any money for booze. Out of my £2 and five shillings wage, I only had five shillings to spend and the rest went to my mum. It cost half a crown for the train and two shillings to get into the Tower so you weren't left with much. Besides, I hadn't come to Blackpool to drink booze, I was there to dance... Oh, and meet boys, of course.

Now, since the disaster with Alan, I'd not had a serious boyfriend. And to be honest, I wasn't all that bothered either (much to Mother's dismay!). Of course I went to the pictures a few times with different boys but it never went any further than them walking me home.

'Did you give him a goodnight kiss?' asked the girls in the mill, teasing me.

'*No!*' I said.

To be honest, I was quite shy and the thought of 'doing it' put the fear of God into me for I hadn't a clue. It wasn't as if we had sex education lessons like today, or my mum had sat me down and told me about the birds and the bees. Back in the day, it wasn't an open subject and even when I was with friends we didn't talk about it, unlike today. And now, as I danced the Foxtrot with this handsome RAF private, although I was enjoying myself, I was shaking like a leaf at the thought of it going any further. Not that I should have been worried for all the men in there were pure gents, plus there was a strict policy in the Tower about how close you danced to your partner. A floorwalker (usually a man) used to stroll around the dancers and, if any pairs were smooching, he would tap the man's shoulder and say, 'Aha, that's enough of that! We don't want any of that.' You were only allowed – well, supposed – to do dances with less bodily contact, like the Foxtrot and the Quick Step.

As the evening went on, I danced with a few more men and I was having the time of my life. But, like all good things, it had to come to an end and 11pm was looming.

'We have to go,' said Dorothy, finding me

on the floor.

'Will I see you next week?' asked an eager young man.

'I'm not sure,' I replied.

As I scurried away with my friends towards the station we talked non-stop about our night.

'It was amazing,' gasped Eva. 'All those men to dance with!'

'He was nice, who you had the last dance with,' Dorothy noted. 'Did you not like him?'

'He was nice enough,' I replied. 'Plenty more where he came from!'

At that, we burst into giggles. It was all innocent fun and we'd have run a mile if any of them had tried anything. And, when we got back on the train, it was even more full than coming out.

'I don't think we should go in that carriage,' I said, pointing. It was full of young men who looked a little bit raucous. And I could even see a few of them kissing girls! 'Come on, this one is safer,' I added, spotting one with mixed couples of an older age.

'I'd be frightened to death if one of them grabbed me for a kiss,' said Mavis.

'Me too!' added Dorothy.

As the train left the platform, we all giggled innocently, already excited about the next week.

From then on, going to the Tower became a regular occurrence and the highlight of my week. It would be the main topic of conversation on a Monday dinnertime in the mill, and again on a Friday dinnertime.

'So, you meeting a lad there?' asked Sissy.

It was common to do this if you'd met a boy the week before that you liked, or, since we'd started going to a dance on a Thursday at the RAF camp at Wheaton, Lancashire, you'd arrange to meet him at the Tower.

'Yes,' I said. 'I'm meeting him outside.'

'Well, you just be careful,' she told me. 'And then make sure you go straight inside!'

'I will,' I smiled.

It was so touching how much she cared. Mum knew I was meeting a boy too as I was quite open and she knew I went to the RAF dances. She didn't bother because I was a good girl and she knew I could be trusted.

But the next day, when I arrived at 7.30pm, he wasn't there.

'Are you going to wait?' asked Dorothy.

'Only for five minutes,' I replied, annoyed that he wasn't already there. I stood outside like a lemon waiting but after half an hour I gave up.

'He never showed up,' I told Dorothy, finding her in the crowd of dancers.

I wasn't that bothered, just more put out that he hadn't waited where we'd arranged. And then, I spotted him dancing!

'I'm sorry,' he said. 'I couldn't remember the time we'd arranged so I thought I'd come in.'

Disgruntled, I just shrugged, telling him I was off to find my mates – I couldn't be bothered with him if he didn't have the decency to wait for me. I was hoping it was a one-off but, when the same thing happened again a few weeks later, I soon realised how complicated men could be.

'I'm not hanging around like a fool, waiting for a boy again,' I told the women at work on the Monday. 'They're nothing but trouble!' said one.

'You mean *yours* is!' added another, as all the older women cracked up laughing. 'There are *some* good things about them!'

'Aye, you're probably right!' she agreed. 'And he's not even that good at that!'

Even though I was now used to the banter flowing, I still blushed when the women's language got colourful.

'Don't worry, there's plenty more fish in the sea,' they told me. 'He weren't worth it, and you're better off without him!'

I knew they were right and, from then on, I was determined just to have fun with my friends.

On 13 December 1952, when I was 16, a group of us had gone to the Tower as usual but it got so packed in there that we started splitting up into pairs and meeting again at the end of the night to catch the train home. So, this particular night, it was Eva and me walking together when two guys approached us.

'Would you care for a dance?' asked one. Small, dark and handsome, he was dressed in a dark suit with a shirt and tie and his hair was styled in the popular DA – a duck's arse, which meant his greased hair was piled high on top and swept back at the sides to form a ridge – and looked very smart and trendy. He introduced himself as Walter Wilson, but, although he oozed charm and charisma, it was his friend Derek who took my eye. He was fair, and I seemed to like that look, as that's what Alan had been and also my uncle Walter, and he also seemed nice. But out of the two of them it was Walter doing all the talking, and, when he asked for my hand and Derek asked Eva, I obliged. Not only would it have been rude to refuse, I didn't see the point as Derek had already taken Eva's hand.

As Walter glided me around the floor, doing the Waltz and the Quick Step, he was very confident and chatting away, telling me he was 19 and in the Army, doing his National Service, and his base was somewhere in Wales, and asking me how often I came to the Tower. I'd never spoken to a man so much! As I've said, I was quite shy. I danced

with boys but I was still very inexperienced –
and I was only 16.

'So, can I walk you back to the train?' he
asked, as the dance came to an end.

'OK,' I replied coyly.

As the four of us walked back to the station,
Walter asked me where I lived and whether
I'd like to write to him. This may seem
forward in today's dating game but back then
it was the norm, especially for boys in the
forces. I didn't want to be rude so I just
agreed and we swapped addresses.

'I'm home again in a few weeks, so we
could meet up,' he said, giving me a peck on
the cheek.

'OK,' I said. 'Goodnight.'

Getting on the train, Eva and me took our
seats and waved to the boys as it pulled out
of the station.

'Are you going to write?' asked Eva.

I shook my head. 'No,' I told her.

If I'm honest, I wasn't that bothered. I
wasn't being cocky, it was just that Walter
hadn't made an impression on me, and I
was enjoying going to the Tower and doing
my own thing.

'I'm not bothered either,' added Eva.

Typical, I thought. *If only Derek had asked
me to dance...*

By the time Monday morning had come
around and I was trekking to the mill in the

cold, Walter was the last thing on my mind.

'Brrrr, it's freezing!' I shivered. 'I can't wait to get in!'

The great thing about working in the mill was the heat. No matter how cold it was outside, or at home, the mill was always boiling from the heat coming from the machines and, the minute you walked in, the heat would just hit you.

'Ah!' I sighed.

There was a good buzz in the mill at this time of year as it was almost Christmas, so people were getting excited for it meant a couple of days off work.

'We usually knock off a bit earlier,' explained Mum.

We finished on Christmas Eve and went back to work the day after Boxing Day but there was no Christmas party or tree up in the mill. The only thing we had was paper chain decorations but we had to be careful where we hung them because of the machinery.

I think that year I probably babysat on Christmas Eve as Mum and Dad would have nipped to the pub for a few drinks. I mean it wasn't like parents today who have tons of presents to wrap and all the food to prepare. Christmas was never a luxurious affair in our house but, year by year, it had got that bit better (especially in comparison to when we were kids) and there was no need for any of us to go to the Ragged School again.

Our Terry was away in the Army, but for the rest of us it was a nice day. We had paper chains looped around the house, but no tree. I think I got a blouse that Christmas and the younger ones were given a couple of toys each; we ate a capon (a large chicken) for dinner.

During the Christmas holidays, I received a letter from Walter.

'Who's that then?' asked Mum, as I ripped open the envelope.

'No one,' I replied. I hadn't given Walter a second thought since we'd met. As I've said, he hadn't made an impression on me and I was happy enough going to the Tower and dancing with other young men. I didn't bother to reply, as I didn't see the point.

Then, in the New Year, Eva and I had gone to Preston, a bigger town less than 10 miles away, on a Saturday afternoon for a shop. Not that we could afford much but we loved looking in the windows or browsing the stores like Marks & Spencer. I was walking up Fishergate, the main shopping road in Preston, when I saw someone walking towards me whom I recognised. It was Walter, the soldier from the Tower who'd written to me over Christmas.

He came right up to me and said, 'Why didn't you answer my letter?'

I didn't know what to say; he looked really hurt and I felt terrible.

'Oh, I'm sorry,' I replied.

Walter chatted for a bit, telling me he was on a short leave. He asked me how I was, and if I wanted to go to the pictures in Preston on Wednesday. There must have been something about him, or perhaps I felt it was such a coincidence bumping into him that I thought I should give it a go, but something made me agree.

'I'll meet you at the bus station at 7.15pm,' he said.

Back then, you didn't have phones, you just arranged a time and a place, then stuck to it.

'He seems nice,' said Eva, as we parted from Walter. 'And more handsome than I remember!'

Back home, I told Mum about what had happened. 'I thought you weren't keen?' she said.

'I wasn't,' I admitted, 'but he seemed nicer than I remembered and I felt bad for not writing.'

I think I told Mavis and Dorothy, my closest friends at the mill, on Monday about meeting Walter on the Wednesday but don't think I mentioned it to anybody else as I couldn't be fussed with all the questions! By clocking-off time on Wednesday, I was surprised how excited I was to meet Walter. After rushing home, I got changed and brushed cotton out of my hair, then shovelled down my tea before flitting for the bus stop.

As promised, Walter was waiting and we walked to the pictures to watch *Apache*, a Western featuring Burt Lancaster. It cost one shilling and sixpence, but I think we paid for ourselves. I was so nervous – I don't think I said two words all night! And, when we walked outside and he pulled me into the doorway and kissed me, my knees went weak, as it was the first time I'd been kissed *like that* and it was amazing!

On cloud nine I floated back to the bus stop, my head dizzy with delight. Walter – who I was now to call 'Walt' – had certainly turned my head.

The next day in the mill, I couldn't hide the smile from my face.

'Someone had a good night!' teased one of the women.

As my cheeks turned crimson, Mavis and Dorothy kept goading me for details.

'So, did he kiss you?' they asked.

'Yes,' I smiled. 'And it was more than a peck!'

'Oh, my goodness!' they shrieked. 'What was it like?'

'I'm not saying!' I laughed. 'It's nice, though.'

I told them that I'd arranged to meet Walt

on Saturday at the Tower. As usual, I was going with my friends but we said we'd meet inside. And, as usual, the place was heaving when suddenly I saw him. Striding towards me in his suit and blue suede shoes, he looked so dapper.

'Fancy getting a drink?' he asked.

'In the bar?' I asked.

Walt smirked. 'Of course.'

'But I'm not old enough to drink and I won't get in,' I explained.

But Walt was confident: 'Just hold my hand and walk in and you'll be fine,' he told me.

And, although my whole body was shaking with nerves no one said a thing as Walt ordered me half a beer.

'Well, this is a first,' I smiled.

By this time, rock and roll was just starting to break through and people were learning how to jive. Bill Haley and Frankie Laine had arrived on the scene. It was an exciting era and you could sense the change in the air. As for me, I could feel myself changing. I felt like I was growing into a woman, as the more I saw of Walt, deep feelings developed that I never knew existed. When he told me he was due to be posted abroad for a few weeks, I decided to invite him round for tea to meet Mum and Dad. As Mum opened the door to him, without even saying hello or introducing himself, Walt said, 'Have you got that kettle on?'

Straight away Mum was taken by him. 'I like him,' she told me. 'He's all right.'

All the family liked him, although Dad never said much about him.

Walt was posted to Holland and our courtship carried on for a while, with him being home for a bit and then posted abroad again. But each time he was home, he used to come and see me and charm Mum with his cheeky banter.

'He's brilliant,' she'd tell me. 'Just the type I like!'

'Tell the kids not to come into the front room and mess it up,' I fretted. 'I've tidied it up for Walt.'

I wanted the best for him and I soon realised it wasn't just Mum who liked him. I was in love, so, when he was posted away to Düsseldorf in Germany for nine whole months, it was torture.

'I'll write every day,' he promised.

I carried on going to the Tower every Saturday but I missed Walt not being there, and some days it was an effort just to get out of bed to go to work, I missed him so much.

'If you don't get up, I'm going to burn this letter!' said Mum, when she tried to get me up one morning.

'I'm up,' I cried. 'Give it me!'

While pining for Walt, I made a new friend who lifted my spirits and helped me cope without him. Jean Fogerty was about the same age as me and I met her through our Sylvia. By then, I was 17 and, with Sylvia being 15, she had finished school and come into the mill (unlike me, she was never against the idea and came straight away, without protest). She had been given a job as a winder, which meant she wound thread onto the spindles, as that's what was needed at the time, so she was working with Jean.

Jean was slim with short dark hair, attractive and swore like a trooper – and I loved her! She was like a breath of fresh air, she was so much fun. The first day Sylvia introduced us one dinnertime, every other word was 'bloody this' and 'bloody that', and I thought she was hilarious! Now, as I've already told you, I had quite a mischievous streak, which had recently been tamed, so meeting Jean was like meeting my partner in crime. We just clicked! Very soon Jean had become a part of our gang, and not only did she sit with us at dinnertime, but she started coming to the Tower with us too. So, it was no surprise the mischievous side of me reared its head again, thanks to Jean. We were a bad combination, as we just wanted to have a laugh together.

'What are you two like?' tutted Mum. 'You're like two peas in a pod!'

One lunchtime, we went out into the yard

and saw one of the young lads out there. Before he had time to move, we'd run up to him, picked him up and lifted him into one of the empty wicker baskets used for bobbins.

'Get off me!' he shouted. He was playing hell! But all Jean and me could do was laugh, and I don't think we even got told off.

'I heard what you and Jean did at lunchtime,' said Sissy, smirking.

'Don't tell my mum!' I pleaded. 'She'll kill me!'

Other times, we would wind up Maggie-Anne. 'You've got a big ball of cotton on your shoes,' Jean would say, so the big woman would bend over and her backside would be sticking up in the air. By the time she had realised and bent back up, we were well and truly gone! Other times we broke her ends, and if the other women saw us they'd just shake their heads and laugh.

'It never gets boring!' sniggered Jean.

We were naughty, really, but it was all harmless fun. Jean was such a good laugh and she took my mind off missing Walt.

He'd be there for a couple of weeks and then be away again for a couple of months, so I'd count down the days when he was due home. One particular time, it was a Friday afternoon, close to clocking-off, and I couldn't wait to finish and go and meet him, when suddenly one of the older ladies –

Mary – came running in.

'Eh, there's a belting soldier outside! You wanna see this soldier. Who's he with?' she cried.

Suddenly, my heart skipped a beat, hoping it was Walt. He sometimes came to meet me at work when he was home, but never in his uniform. Nipping outside, I had a sneaky look and saw it was him and, oh my, he did look handsome in his khaki uniform and beret!

'It's Walt,' I told everyone.

'He's a bit of all right!' cried Mary. 'You've done all right there.'

I chuckled to myself. Mary was in her 30s and married, but the women in there were brazen in a good way. Ten minutes later, at 5.30pm, it was time for home, and as I walked outside with Mary, towards Walt, she asked him, 'Eh, Walt, have you got any dockers [ends of cigarettes]?' I was so embarrassed as she sounded so common but I knew I was just being silly because I was with Walt. He laughed it off but the next time he came to pick me up he had some dockers in an envelope for her.

And, although it was lovely having him home for Christmas that year in 1953, there was another buzz of excitement escalating around the mill.

'So, you ready for the Christmas party?' asked the women at dinnertime. 'I think we're having it with Cherry Tree, in their canteen.'

The year before, we hadn't had a party so, as the date got closer, the excitement was building and it was all the women talked about in the mill.

'So, what you wearing?' asked Jean, the day before at dinnertime. The party was on a Saturday night.

'I bought a black and white checked taffeta dress from town,' I replied.

'Ooh,' she teased. 'All right for bloody some, eh?'

The next night, our Sylvia and me walked down and met Jean, Mavis and Dorothy. Mum didn't come – I think she may have been babysitting, as perhaps Dad was out, too. I don't think I ever asked why, if I'm honest. We had party food and pop (but no alcohol) and music and dancing too. And, typical of Jean and me, we went for a snoop around the mill and ended up in the women's toilets, messing about doing good-ness knows what, when a brick from the wall fell and whacked me on the head.

'Ow!' I cried.

'Oh no, are you all right?' asked Jean, worried.

'No, that hurt!' I replied, rubbing my head and seeing a speck of blood. 'I think I'd better go home.'

I grabbed our Sylvia and the pair of us walked home. Mum took one look at me and said I needed to go to the hospital, so, while Sylvia watched the kids, she and I got a bus to Queen's Park.

I felt it was a little over the top but Mum wanted to be sure.

'What happened?' the doctor asked.

'A brick fell on my head,' I replied.

Mum rolled her eyes. 'Don't ask!' she said. 'No doubt you and that Jean were up to no good.'

As a precaution, the doctor wanted to keep me in for the night: 'Come back tomorrow,' he told Mum.

As a nurse tucked me into a bed, Mum leaned over, kissed my forehead and said, 'I love you.' I was 17 and it was the first time I'd ever heard her say it. In a funny sort of way I was grateful for that brick hitting me, as I never doubted for one second she didn't, but it was still lovely to hear she did.

And the next day I was allowed home in time for Christmas. It was wonderful having Walt with me over the festive period and I felt even more grown up when, that year, aged 17, we went to the pub on Christmas Eve after we'd finished work at 3.30pm and I think we all went out on New Year's Eve too. But I wouldn't have had much to drink, if I drank at all, because we didn't have the money.

As we counted down to 1954, I felt blissfully happy and lucky. I had a lovely fella, a brilliant family (we might have had the odd squabble but we all got on really well as a rule), great mates and a job – and one that I actually liked (well, I liked what camaraderie it brought, I should say) – so life, I thought, was pretty good. But, a few weeks into the New Year, Walt was once again posted to Düsseldorf, in Germany, for nine months.

'You're kidding!' I sighed. 'That's such a long time.'

'I'll write every day,' he promised.

And, although it was lovely hearing from him, it just made my heart pine for him all the more.

'He'll soon be home,' said Jean. She kept my spirits high by making me laugh on a daily basis. And, of course, we still went dancing in the Tower. But it was tough.

A few months later, when Walt said he was going to send me a catalogue, I wondered what he was on about. And a couple of weeks later, I opened a parcel with a German catalogue inside and a letter from Walt too. Still confused, as I read his letter, I suddenly shrieked with joy.

'Oh, my goodness, Walt has bought me an engagement ring,' I cried. 'We are getting engaged!'

I was 18 years old. Today, that probably

seems exceptionally young, but then it was the norm as it meant I could be married in a year or two. And, although there was no going down on a bended knee or asking my father for my hand, I didn't care. I was just ecstatic to be engaged.

I'm not sure who was in our house when I shrieked with joy, but, the minute Mum walked in, I told her the good news.

'Congratulations,' she said. 'He's a good one!'

Again, I don't think there was any big celebration at home. I know my dad was pleased too and so were my siblings, more so that they could be bridesmaids!

Walt had sent the catalogue so I could see the ring he had bought. Well, I *say* bought, it cost £10 and 10 shillings but he got it on the never-never so he was paying it off in bits. It was a red stone with two little diamonds on the side and very pretty it was, too.

'Not bad,' said Mum.

'He's posted it to his mum's so I need to go and pick it up,' I said.

So, the next day, I caught the bus to Lytham and I couldn't wait to put my ring on. *I'm engaged,* I kept thinking to myself all the way. So, imagine my surprise – and horror – when his mum answered the door to me wearing *my* ring.

'I opened the package and wanted to check it was OK,' she said.

Stunned, I took it from her and came straight home.

'*What?*' cried Mum. 'She had your engagement ring on?'

'*Yes!*' I fumed. 'She'd unwrapped the parcel and put it on – I was speechless.'

But I soon forgot about that, come Monday morning as I was dying to get in to work and share my good news.

'Congratulations!' screeched Mavis and Dorothy.

'That's bloody great!' cheered Jean.

'I'm really happy for you,' said Sissy.

'That's great, kid!' said the other older women. 'You deserve it.'

Everyone was chuffed to bits. I was on cloud nine and felt a huge sense of relief. As I've said, there was a lot of pressure at that time to get married, especially at a young age. No one wanted to be a spinster or fall pregnant out of wedlock. That had happened to a friend of mine. Now, looking back, I feel really dreadful, for we had disowned her. She was only 18 and had to get married because she was expecting. I was lucky that I hadn't been forced to marry Walt but I'd chosen to do so.

Showing off my ring, I was ecstatic. 'Very nice,' everyone cooed. There was a genuine, sincere affection from the women. 'Must have cost him a bob or two.' We all knew it wasn't an expensive ring as none of us could afford one, but I didn't care: it was what it represented that mattered to me.

Walt and I decided to get married on 17 December 1955 at St Andrew's Church. But, although I couldn't wait to be a wife, I knew it meant I'd have to leave my old life behind, as he wanted me to move to Lytham.

'Walt says I won't need to work once we're married,' I told Mum.

'Oh, it's all right for some!' she smirked.

But, although the thought of not having to work in the mill (or anywhere else) was quite appealing, the idea of leaving all my friends and family broke my heart. As the months counted down to my big day, it wasn't the drama it is today when someone gets married. Walt and I saved up for a bottom drawer, a common expression then, and I remember people bought us towels and blankets. My last day in the mill was the Friday, the day before my wedding. I didn't have a leaving do and I just got a couple of cards.

'Good luck, love!' cheered the women, as they each gave me a big hug.

Fighting back the tears, I couldn't believe I wouldn't be going back there again. Of course, I was excited to be married, but I was grieving for the life I'd lose. I may never have wanted to go in the mill, but, three years on, I didn't want to leave either. The mill had been so good to me and I was going to miss it more than I ever would have imagined.

After honeymooning in London, Walt and I moved to a house in Lytham, St Annes. I did bits of work before having our three boys Steven, Stewart and Andrew, and then I worked for the book company Holt & Jacksons for 26 years as a classifier for the books. Sadly, Walt and I split up in 1975; it was just a breakdown of the marriage.

Although I now see Lytham as my home, I missed the mill and everyone in there for a long time. The only person I kept in touch with was Jean. She was still the same lively character but, sadly, I haven't seen her for 20 years because we lost contact. I was sad to hear the mills were closing, and, although it was hard work, the people in there were the salt of the earth and I was proud to work with them. As I've said, I'm not sure if I'd have wanted my sons to have gone in the mill but only because the work was hard and, like any mother, you always want better for your kids. If they'd wanted to, I wouldn't have objected, though. For me, the mill was one of the best times of my life, and the memories of those days I'll cherish forever.

Acknowledgements

I'd like to give a special thanks to Audrey Waddington, Doris Porter, Marjorie Wilkinson and Maureen Wilson for sharing their life stories with me, and to all the other women who came forward to volunteer theirs too. Thanks to everyone who contributed information, or offered to help, especially my dad, David Johnson. I'd also like to thank my mum and dad, my family and friends for their constant encouragement and support.

The publishers hope that this book has given you enjoyable reading. Large Print Books are especially designed to be as easy to see and hold as possible. If you wish a complete list of our books please ask at your local library or write directly to:

Magna Large Print Books
Magna House, Long Preston,
Skipton, North Yorkshire.
BD23 4ND

This Large Print Book, for people
who cannot read normal print,
is published under the auspices of

THE ULVERSCROFT FOUNDATION